D1352210

BANDIT

A DAUGHTER'S MEMOIR

MOLLY BRODAK

ICON

Published in the UK in 2016
by Icon Books Ltd,
Omnibus Business Centre,
39–41 North Road,
London N7 9DP
email: info@iconbooks.com
www.iconbooks.com

First published in the USA in 2016
by Grove Atlantic, 154 West 14th Street,
New York, N.Y. 10011

Sold in the UK, Europe and Asia
by Faber & Faber Ltd, Bloomsbury House,
74–77 Great Russell Street,
London WC1B 3DA
or their agents

Distributed in the UK, Europe and Asia
by Grantham Book Services,
Trent Road, Grantham NG31 7XQ

Distributed in Australia and New Zealand
by Allen & Unwin Pty Ltd,
PO Box 8500, 83 Alexander Street,
Crows Nest, NSW 2065

Distributed in South Africa
by Jonathan Ball, Office B4, The District,
41 Sir Lowry Road, Woodstock 7925

Distributed in India
by Penguin Books India,
7th Floor, Infinity Tower – C, DLF Cyber
City, Gurgaon 122002, Haryana

Portions of this book originally appeared in
LIT, the *Fanzine,* and *Granta.*

The epigraph to this book is an excerpt from "XVII. Sometimes
above the gross and palpable things of this diurnal sphere wrote
Keats (Not a doctor but he danced as an apothecary) who also
recommended strengthening the intellect by making up one's mind
about nothing" from *The Beauty of the Husband* by Anne Carson.
Published by Jonathan Cape and reprinted by permission of
The Random House Group Ltd and Anne Carson. All rights reserved.

The Friedrich Nietzsche quote that appears on page 168 is an excerpt
from *Ecce Home: How One Becomes What Is* by Friedrich Nietzsche,
translated with notes by R. J. Hollingdale, introduction by Michael
Tanner (Penguin Classics 1979, Revised 1992). Translation copyright
© R. J. Hollingdale, 1979. New introduction and text revisions copyright
© Michael Tanner, 1992. Reproduced by permission of Penguin Books Ltd

The Walter Benjamin quote that appears on page 260 is an excerpt
from "On Some Motifs in Baudelaire" from *Illuminations* by
Walter Benjamin, translated by Harry Zohn, English translation
copyright © 1968 by Harcourt Brace Jovanovich, Inc.

ISBN: 978-178578-103-2

Text copyright © 2016 Molly Brodak

The author has asserted her moral rights.

No part of this book may be reproduced in any form, or by any
means, without prior permission in writing from the publisher.

Printed and bound in the UK by Clays Ltd, St Ives plc

For Boo

READING BOROUGH LIBRARIES	
Askews & Holts	
920	£14.99

Fiction forms what streams in us.
Naturally it is suspect.
—Anne Carson, *The Beauty of the Husband*

1

I was with my dad the first time I stole something.

It was a little booklet of baby names. I was seven and I devoured word lists: dictionaries, vocabulary sheets, menus. The appeal of this string of names, their pleasing shapes and neat order, felt like a puzzle impossible to solve. I couldn't ask for it but I couldn't leave it. I pressed it to my chest as we walked out of Kroger. It was pale blue with the word BABY spelled out in pastel blocks above a stock photo of a smiling white baby in a white diaper. I stood next to Dad, absorbed in page one, as he put the bags in the trunk of his crappy gold Chevette, and he stopped when he saw it. At first he said nothing. He avoided my eyes. He just pressed hard into my back and marched me back into the store, to the lane we'd left, plucked the stupid booklet out of my hand, and presented it to the cashier.

"My daughter stole this. I apologize for her." He beamed a righteous look over a sweep of people nearby. The droopy cashier winced and muttered that it was OK, chuckling mildly. Then stooping over me he shouted, "Now you apologize. You will never do this again." The cold anger in his face was edged with some kind of glint I didn't recognize. As he gripped my shoulders he was almost smiling. I remember his shining eyes above me and the high ceiling of the gigantic store and the brightness of it. I am sure I cried but I don't remember. I do remember an acidic boiling in my chest and a rinse of sweaty cold on my skin, disgusted with my own desire and what it did, how awful all of us felt now because of me. I didn't steal again until I was a teenager, when he was in prison.

2

Dad robbed banks one summer.

He robbed the Community Choice Credit Union on 13 Mile Road in Warren.

He robbed the Warren Bank on 19 Mile Road.

He robbed the NBD Bank in Madison Heights.

He robbed the NBD Bank in Utica.

He robbed the TCF Bank on 10 Mile Road in Warren.

He robbed the TCF Bank on 14 Mile Road in Clawson, where I would open my first checking account when I turned seventeen. That's the one with the little baskets of Dum-Dums at each window and the sour herb smell from the health food store next door.

He robbed the Credit Union One on 15 Mile Road in Sterling Heights.

He robbed the Michigan First Credit Union on Gratiot in Eastpointe.

He robbed the Comerica Bank on 8 Mile and Mound. That was as close as he got to the Detroit neighborhood he grew up in, Poletown East, about ten miles south.

He robbed the Comerica Bank inside a Kroger on 12 Mile and Dequindre. All of the shoppers gliding by as Dad passed a note to the teller in silence: "This is a robbery, I have a gun."

He robbed the Citizens State Bank on Hayes Road in Shelby Township. Afterward the cops caught up with him finally, at Tee-J's Golf Course on 23 Mile Road. They peeked into his parked car: a bag of money and his disguise in the backseat, plain as day. He was sitting at the bar, drinking a beer and eating a hot ham sandwich.

I was thirteen that summer. He went to prison for seven years after a lengthy trial, delayed by constant objections and rounds of him firing his public defenders. After his release he lived a normal life for seven years, and then robbed banks again.

3

There: see? Done with the facts already. The facts are easy to say; I say them all the time. They leave me out. They cover over the trouble like a lid. This isn't about them.

This is about whatever is cut from the frame of narrative. The fat remnants, broke bones, gristle, untender bits. Me, and Mom, and my sister, and him, the actual him beyond the Bandit version on the evening news.

I see my little self there, under the stories. It's 1987 and I am set between my parents like a tape recorder: Dad on the couch, fixed to the TV, Mom leaning in from the kitchen, me in between on the clumpy beige carpet with spelling worksheets. I am writing out the word *people*, watching the word slip off of my pencil lead, but then I start listening so carefully that I cease to see what I'm doing. Mom is grumbling *what do I know* and *what is wrong with you* again and again and Dad is talking over her steadily and laughing in a friendly way without taking his eyes off the game. More words are forming under my hand in an uneasy cursive. My sister, age nine, stomps through the scene and out the back door, slamming it for all of us. Mom and Dad's voices rise but are cut off at a strange cracking sound. We all turn to the picture window to see my sister smashing walnut-sized white decorative rocks from the neighbor's garden with a hammer on the concrete patio. She pulls the hammer as far above her shoulder as she can and brings it down on a rock, splitting it into dust and flying shards. Dad looks back to the TV. Mom rushes out the door and now my sister hugs the weapon to her chest; Mom appears and rips it away from her. I am recording this so carefully that I don't see it while it is happening.

Where am I when I am listening and watching so carefully?

At the dinner table I am watching my parents' simmering volley crescendo from pissy fork drops to plate slams to stomps off and squeals away, my sister biting into the cruel talk just to feel included, me just watching as if on the living room side of a television screen: I could see them but they could definitely not see me. I squashed my wet veggies around on my plate, eyes fixed to their drama, exactly as I'd do in front of *Scooby Doo* or *G.I. Joe*. I could sleep, I could squirm off, I could hum, dance, or even talk, safe in their blind spot. I could write, I discovered, and no one could hear me.

One survival technique is to *get small*. When resources are thin and you must stay where you are, as you must as a child, it helps to stay invisible. This family, collected together occasionally in one house, or more often, in various split combinations of children and adults, netted around me like a loose constellation of problems. On my small ground, as if in another country, I was not a problem. I kept quiet, was good and smart and secret and neat, reading and playing alone, catching bugs, collecting rocks, reading and drawing. And I wanted to become even less, a nothing, because I thought they could all at least have that, this one non-problem in the house, to not yell and not cry, to sweep the kitchen and pick up the thrown things and secretly restore order to whole fought-apart rooms and even to sometimes sing softly, happily, maybe for them to hear. I have kept quiet about all this my whole life.

4

Suddenly one day, like a membrane breached: before, Dad was like all other dads and then not. We sat together in a booth at the Big Boy, the winter-black windows reflecting back a weak pair of us, and I idly asked him what recording studios are like and how they work. I was something like eleven, and I had a cloudy notion that it would be exciting and romantic to work in a recording studio, to help create music but not have to play it. He fluttered his eyes upward, as he often did, and answered without hesitation.

He told me about the equipment, and how bands work with producers, how much money sound engineers make, and what their schedules are like. Details, I started to realize, he could not possibly know. Some giant drum began turning behind my eyes.

I could see he was lying. Something changed around his eyes when he spoke, a kind of haze or color shift, and I could always see it from then on.

As he talked, I felt my belief, something I didn't know was there until I felt it moving, turn away from him until it was gone, and I was just alone, nodding and smiling. But what a marvel to watch him construct bullshit and to finally see it right. He stopped in the middle of a sentence about groupies.

"Finish your chicken," he said. I stared at him in silence. His face went blank as a wall.

"I'm full thank you," I said cheerily, trying to hide my thoughts. I watched the new man in his seat. He withdrew money from his wallet for the bill and watched me back. A barrier of pressure between us he would not cross. He'd lost his mark.

5

From under the bed I pull a plastic bin stuffed with note-books: thousands of pages of writings, days I set down, starting at age eight. I would give anything to see the artifacts again—the actual days I spent with my family—to turn them over in my hands and catalogue their facts with my grown-up faculties. Who doesn't wish for this? Now those days exist only in this bin of paper versions, each entry skewed in the grasp of a child, absent of context.

The earliest diary is a black-and-white, static-print composition book. The beginning pages are covered in unicorn and rainbow drawings and sketches of bulbous fancy dresses done in crayon and neon-colored pencils. Then some pages stuck in from school writing activities:

Shoes

 By Molly

I just got new sandals.
I have grils black high tops to.
My Shoes are always filled with
sand.

Other pages about puddles or balloons or Halloween are happy and fine, with plenty of exclamation points and normal childhood engagement with the world. I read "Shoes" over and over. I leave it next to me while I pile the rest of the diaries onto my bed, searching farther. My eyes get caught on the *By Molly* a few times until I let myself look at the page again. I have been ignoring myself for so long. All of this personhood here, catalogued in plodding blindness and thrown into a bin and hidden. *My Shoes are always filled with sand.*

I open the composition book again. The first real entry is dated June 25, 1988.

Today nothing is pland. Well I don't kno. Yesderday I played where the tree got cut down and mom said its a hot summer. I put food out for farries but it is still here today. My sister got dropped off at dinner. She was mad and didnt talk. She cried and turned red and then stromed outside and said she running away. I ate her plate tuna casaroll. We looked for

her she was under the pine tree. She didn't talk.
She only just scramed I hate you. Today Im don't
care what she does.

Tiny squares of Swiss cheese and mini marshmallows for
dessert, I remember that, putting food out for fairies. I don't
remember the rest of this. At that point I was old enough to
see that our survival was threadbare compared to the other
kids I knew, which explains the remarks about stealing my
sister's portion of tuna casserole as soon as she *stromed* away,
and the feeling of almost sickening marvel at new shoes in the
other entry, which seemed too nice for me. And I remember
my sister grating against Mom and me, the feeling of grating
in my chest when we were together, that exact verb, *grating*.
I kept turning away and away, *today Im don't care, today Im
don't care,* but the grating stayed.

Michigan did see a hot summer in 1988. And it was the
last year we'd all live together as a family: Mom, Dad, sister,
me. I look at the bin of diaries again, feeling overwhelmed.
There's so much to learn there, so much I don't know about
my family.

I didn't know Dad gambled. Sports betting mostly, on
football, baseball, or college basketball, point spreads, totals,
any angle. Bookies, calls to Vegas, two or three TVs at once.

I want to say plainly everything I didn't know. I have a
little of it now, and I want to hold it up and out. I can't help
but hold it up and out.

I knew there were little paper slips and crazy phone calls and intense screaming about sports games—more intense than seemed appropriate—but it only added up to a private tension orbiting around him, buffeting us away. In the dark, I grew up.

The last entry in the black-and-white composition book from 1988 says:

No one home. Today I went

It ends there.

6

Sports betting is so different from card games or other gambling because the player doesn't actually *play* the game he's betting on. His "game" is in the analysis of its information—knowing which players might secretly be hurt or sick, which refs favor which teams, the particular mood of one stadium over another, the specific combination of one pitcher with a certain kind of weather—and the synthesis of hunches, superstitions, wishes, and loyalties. Beyond that, there are the odds the bookies are offering, which reflect what everyone else is predicting, also a factor to weigh for or against. A perfect game for someone who thinks he's smarter than everyone else.

Before Detroit built big casinos downtown there was Windsor Casino right across the border, so there was always blackjack, too. But nobody knows much else about this—my mom, my sister, his coworkers, his brothers and sisters—no one saw his gambling, no one was invited to come along, to share strategies, or even to wish him luck. It was totally private. Mom's experience of his gambling came to her only in cold losses: an empty savings account, the car suddenly gone, bills and debts, threatening phone calls. Sometimes he'd come home with broken ribs, or a broken nose not to be discussed. The rare big win must have been wasted immediately in private, usually on more gambling, or something showy and useless like a new watch for himself. Or, of course, his debts, eternal debts.

Outcomes shake out fast in gambling. In real life, big risks take years to reveal themselves, and the pressure of choosing a career, a partner, a home, a family, a whole identity, might overwhelm an impatient man, one who values his own control, not fate's. He will either want all the options out of a confused greed—hoarding overlapping partners, shallow hobbies, new alternate selves—or he will refuse them all, risking nothing. And really, the first option is the second option. Keeping a few girlfriends or wives around effectively dismisses a true relationship with any one of them. Being a good, hardworking dad and a criminal at the same time is a way of choosing neither.

Besides, an addict is already faithfully committed to something he prioritizes above all else. Gambling addiction, particularly, is easy to start; it usually requires no elaborate or illegal activities, no troublesome ingestion of substances, and programs the body using its own chemicals: adrenaline, endorphins, spikes of joy. Only once did I see Dad's face after a night of gambling. I was eight. It was early Sunday morning, before

Mom or my sister were awake. I was belly down on the carpet with a small arrangement of Legos, singing to myself, light still gray in the living room. The front door unlocked and opened and I looked, petrified with fear. Dad, obscure in silhouette, but shining somehow, his hair wet, face wet. Stony expression: eyes set steady, mouth drawn in. His shirt hung heavy on him. I stared from the floor, silent. He didn't see me. He turned, still blank, and disappeared down the hall. A dark V of sweat running down the back of his shirt. Quietly I turned back to my Lego arrangement, looking at it, but not seeing, quiet.

What did I know about gambling? Even as I grew older, I avoided sports, avoided casinos and card games, avoided even the lottery. As an adult I wasn't equipped to understand him, having no understanding of gambling.

At first I thought gambling was about chance, just the possibility to make something out of nothing, to multiply money just through pure cleverness. He'd like that: something from nothing.

And that is the first charm. But I know now that gambling is about certainty, not chance. Outcomes, whether win or lose, are certain, immediate, and clear. In other words, there *will* be a result to any one bet, a point in time when this risk will be unequivocally resolved and the skill and foresight of the gambler can be perfectly measured. A shot of adrenaline will issue into the bloodstream, win *or* lose. It's not messy, not indefinite or uncontrollable, like love or people, things Dad labored to control. The space of gambling absorbs its players away from uncertainty, the unknown: how the world works.

7

My dad was born August 19, 1945, in a refugee camp set up for the survivors just liberated from Nazi concentration camps. This is how he first lived: being carried by his mother, in secret, while she worked silently as a slave for the Nazis in Kempten.

The previous year his mother and father and five siblings were moved out of their home in Szwajcaria, Poland, by the Nazis and forced to board a train. My Aunt Helena, a few years older than my dad, told me she remembers the train. She recalls their mom, Stanislawa, hopping off the train when it stopped to hunt for wood to start a cooking fire. Stanislawa's parents and three of her siblings had died a few years before in Siberia, having been shipped there to cut trees for the Russian supply. "The trees would shatter if they hit the ground because it was so cold. No one had enough clothes or food, so most people died there," Aunt Helena told me in a recent letter replying to my inquiries about our family history. She has memories of their life during the war, "but they don't seem real," she told me. She remembers the mood of the train: the animal-like panic any time the train stopped, the worry of the adults, and her worry when her mother would disappear. They were taken to the Dachau concentration camp, where my grandfather was beaten and interrogated daily because they suspected him of being a partisan, like his brothers.

My dad's dad was separated from the family. The rest of them lived and worked together, hoping he'd be returned.

After a few months all of them were transferred to a subcamp in Kempten, Germany, where they worked the farm that fed the captives. This is where my grandmother became pregnant with my father. She hid her pregnancy because she was afraid she'd be forced to abort it, so she worked like everyone else and hid her body. Everyone had to work to be fed, even the children and the sick. My aunt remembers little about this time, and won't say much. "There were horrors every day," she says. I don't press her. The war was over in April and my dad was born in August.

After the war they were moved to a refugee camp while trying to find a way out of Germany. My grandfather felt strongly that they should move to Australia, since he liked the idea of working a homestead and living freely, as a farmer. But a few months before they were to leave, he died, and Australia no longer welcomed a widow with five children. They were offered a passage to America through a Catholic sponsorship program, and they took it. My dad's first memories were of this ship: troop transport, cold and gray all around, the sea and metal smell.

They arrived at Ellis Island on December 4, 1951, and Dad's name was changed from Jozef to Joseph. They traveled by train to Detroit. Their sponsor took them to St. Albertus Church, on the corner of St. Aubin and Canfield Streets, on the other side of I-75 from Wayne State University, an area that used to be called Poletown. They lived on the top floor of the adjacent school, built in 1916, until my grandma found work in the cafeteria of the *Detroit News* and rented an apartment for them. Now St. Albertus, no longer a parish as of 1990, stands among abandoned buildings and urban prairie.

Inspired by the family history illuminated by my aunt, I emailed Dad asking him to tell me about his life growing up in Detroit. I had no idea where he was born, and I had no inkling of the incredible ordeal his family shuffled through. He'd never told me any of this. Was it shame? Would he even reply? Quickly he wrote back to say he'd write me a letter, two letters in fact, since he was sure he wouldn't be able to fit it all in one envelope. I waited a month, two months: it wasn't like him. I thought maybe he was sick or worse. Eventually it came—he'd gotten in trouble at his job, he said, for disobeying an order, and had been in solitary confinement for the past few weeks.

The first letter, written on yellow lined paper, was long and cheery. I was suspicious. I've always been both suspicious and suspicious of my suspicion when listening to Dad. What if it wasn't all lies this time? What if he let me in—would I be strong enough to follow? But mostly I knew it would be what it was: an innocuous and slightly heroic vision of himself, his official story, nothing deeper.

He described the neighborhood, a tight-knit, mini Eastern Europe: small blocks of varied ethnicities grouped around their churches, family-owned shops, and split homes. They were terribly poor, living off charity and the small salary that his mom made washing dishes in the cafeteria of the *Detroit News* office downtown. He described her as "superstitiously religious." Every day before school he attended service at St. Albertus, and also on Sundays, leaving only Saturdays without church. His whole world was built on the church—his family, his neighborhood, his education, his citizenship in this country. When they did move out of the school, they lived only a few blocks away. He said he was almost never too far away to hear the church bells chime every fifteen minutes. He said he loved the church. The overwhelming detail of the stained glass, the painted ceiling, the enormous organ, the grand, formal rituals—all of it must have been a steady comfort to him, to all of them, in a new country.

It was nice to hear, I must admit, and it made sense. I didn't much see the impression of the Catholic Church on him, but for his love of luxury. It contrasted with the moral tone of my upbringing by Mom: the blue-collar, midwestern work ethic that identifies laziness, indulgence, and shortcuts as serious sins, having nothing in common with Catholicism besides guilt as a motivational technique. Luxury disgusted me. It all seemed false, however real the materials, however deep the ostentation, or honest the funding—it was all predicated on the notion that money itself meant something *big*, was glorious. I know if I had grown up as poor as my dad I would most likely see this differently.

Dad's mom eventually remarried, to an older Lithuanian man whose money helped the family enormously. They moved into a real house, out of the fleabag apartments they'd been moving through, and he suddenly had a stepdad. He would only describe his stepdad as "crabby." His brothers fought with him regularly, and so he kept his distance. In one letter he tells me his stepdad carved for him a toy wooden rifle—the one and only present he ever gave him—and how much he loved it. My dad devoted one whole letter to describing him, the houses they lived in, and which of his siblings moved out when. The second letter is colder and hesitant. Dad was the last to leave home. I can see him there, with his mother to whom he could hardly relate, and his distant stepfather, a non-dad, for whom there was no real role in his life. He turned inward. I know how that works. Perhaps he felt abandoned or lonely.

By the time he was leaving elementary school his neighborhood started to change too. As the Polish immigrants moved to Hamtramck and other white neighbors moved to the suburbs, black folks replaced them—people whom my father had, until this point, never met. "With them," he wrote, "came crime and drugs. It was demoralizing, to see these strange black people that I previously saw at a distance now living next door to us." His childhood world, as small and culturally monolithic as most childhood worlds, was cracking open. The Polish family on the corner moved out and the property became a post for drug dealers in just a few months. The family-owned businesses he grew up with closed or moved. Tensions boiled. Newly established black-owned businesses were torched. Vigilante "patrols" were established to keep one group away from another group's street. White immigrant families abandoned entire blocks together, chasing hopes for reestablishing homogenous neighborhoods elsewhere. This is the story all over Detroit throughout the fifties and sixties, White Flight, how abandonment began to build a "white noose" around the city. In his letter he says most people do not have a "good reason" to dislike black people, but he does. I am ashamed by this and I wonder what potential warmth was cut from his personality in his turn toward hatred of his neighbors.

He stayed in Detroit until he left for Vietnam in the midseventies. When he returned, he moved to a flat just a few blocks away from St. Albertus with his first wife and their daughter, my half-sister. And every letter he has ever written to me about his life story ends there. Perhaps this is just practical—he thinks I know the rest of the story. But, this is important. This part of his life—everything before he met my mom—this is the part he can present as wholesome. He was innocent then, not a criminal yet—or at least, could *say* he was innocent then. *All* the letters end there.

8

I know my dad feels a hole where his father should be. Everyone in his family knew his father except him. His first letter to me starts with "You probably know that if my father had lived, my life would have turned out much differently." On the surface I know he means they would have moved to Australia. But there is more to it. I don't think he really knows how well I understand this.

I've seen a few photos of him when he was a child. One I remember hanging in a frame with other photos—he was a child and someone was holding him; a man, possibly his stepfather, was standing with his mother and siblings in front of a house and landscape. He had a serious face but a tree trunk had aligned just perfectly behind him so it looked like it was growing straight out of his head. My sister and I used to look at this and laugh about it. I'd look closely at this small black-and-white photo, sad and stiff, but laugh at it.

One photo I own—it is a new and glossy reprint of a photo and I'm not sure how I came to have it. Probably I stole it from a photo album at some point. Dad's family is all clustered around his father's fresh grave. They must be in Germany, at the camp where Dad was born. His oldest sister is standing, looking down at the grave, next to a wooden cross at the head of the grave, a small photo of his father's face nailed to the center. His two brothers kneel at the foot of the grave, looking with sad, small faces at whoever was taking the photo. Worn faces, especially for children. His other sister, next to them, is looking into the camera, brows knitted, hands pressed in prayer. She looks serious and intelligent. And then, in the middle, his mother, kneeling in black, holding Dad. His mother looks directly into the camera, chin down, mouth open a little as if she was just saying something. She is pretty and tough, with high, wide cheekbones like mine. Dad is just a baby, wrapped all in black. He is looking somewhere else entirely. His face is neutral. Pudgy cheeks bulging downward. He is the only one there who doesn't understand.

The background is just gray, vague hills. Ghostly gray blankness. I keep the photo facedown in a folder with the letters he has written to me. It confronts me. Who would have taken this photo of a family in their most private and serious moment of grief, not posing but mourning next to their father's grave? And is this what I am doing now in writing about my family?

My dad's father's name was Kazimierz and he was a farmer, famous for breaking horses in the river Strypa. His parents were killed in Poland in 1941. Before he died he received news that his four brothers had been executed for treason. He died from a heart attack on his thirty-sixth birthday in March, 1948, when my dad was two years old.

Aren't we together on this, Dad, together on missing our dads, and what it has done to you and me? You left an unknowable self behind, with us, your cover story, your dupes, and I kept following. And I'm still following, somehow more than ever, in love with this trouble, this difficult family, in love with my troubled mom and sister and you too, maybe most of all you, the unknowable one.

9

From the window of the cab our beachfront hotel approached like a dream, as wrong as a dream, and I felt sickly overwhelmed with the luxury of the fantastic palm trees and clean arched doorways. This could not be right. I hung my mouth open a while in joy and suspicion as we left the cab, for him to see. He made a goofy roundabout pointing sweep to the door and said "Lezz go," goofily, like he did. Thinking about it now, the hotel was probably nothing special, maybe even cheap, but I couldn't have known.

This was the longest period of time we spent alone together as father and daughter. I was nine or ten and he'd brought me to Cancun, an unlikely place to take a child on a summer vacation for no particular reason. He had a habit of taking vacations with just me or just my sister, never both of us together, and never with Mom, even when they were married.

I imagine we never went anywhere all together as a family because Mom and Dad usually hated each other, but I didn't get why my sister and I couldn't go somewhere together. Now, reasoning it out, I run through a spectrum of guesses: on the practical end, there is cost and scheduling logistics, and on the other end, the darker end, there is purposeful isolation.

During the day he would leave me. I'd wake up and find a key and a note atop some money: *Have fun! Wear sunscreen!* I'd put on my nubby yellow bathing suit and take myself to the beach or the small intensely chlorinated pool and try hard to have a fun vacation as instructed.

What was he doing? Was there somewhere nearby to gamble? There must have been. Or was there a woman he met? He'd return in the evening and take me to eat somewhere nearby. He always ordered a hamburger and a Coke for me without looking at the menu, even though I hated hamburgers and Coke. Mom wouldn't let me drink soda, and it seemed important to him to break her rules.

"*Hahmm-borrr-gaysa,*" he'd say to the waiter, childishly drawing out the words and gesturing coarsely as if the waiter were near-blind and deaf, "and *Coca-Colé!*" he'd finish, pro-nouncing the "cola" part with a silly "Olé!" paired with an insulting bottle-drinking mime. He was condescending to waiters everywhere like big shots often are, but especially here. "This is the only word you need to know," he told me from across the dark booth. "*Hamburguesa.*" I tamped down my disgust with obliging laughs, since clearly this show was for me. I did not recognize his gold chain and ring. I watched him carefully, waiting for a time when we'd say real things to each other.

I didn't tell him that I liked my days there, on the beach, alone like a grown-up. But anxious. I knew the untethered feeling I liked was not right for me yet. If he asked, I would have told him about my days lying on a blue towel, just lying there for hours, burning pink in the sun, listening while two Mexican teenage girls talked next to me, oblivious to my eaves-dropping, alternating between Spanish and English. They talked about how wonderful it would be to be born a *gringa,* the kind of house they'd live in, what their boyfriends would look like, and how their daddies would spoil them with cars and clothes and fantastic birthday parties.

One of the days he didn't leave, he waited for me to wake up and took me to a Mayan ruin site. Before the tour we foreigners drew in automatically to giant steep steps of a pyramid and began to climb. It was so soaking hot, and I felt so young and small. The other tourists seemed to have such trouble climbing. I bounded up the old blocks, turning to the wide mush of treetops below and smiling. Dad down below. I waved to him but he wasn't looking.

We were herded up for the tour and kids my age and even older were already whining. I couldn't imagine complaining even half as much as my peers did. It frightened me, the way they said what they wanted. *Hungry* and *tired* and *thirsty* and *bored* and *ugh, Dad, can we go?* At the edge of the cenote nearby a tour guide described how the Mayans would sacrifice young women here by tossing them in; "girls about your age," he said and pointed at me. The group of tourists around us chuckled uncomfortably but I straightened up.

I rested on a boulder carved into a snake's head, wearing the only hat I owned as a child, a black-and-neon tropical-print baseball hat I am certain came from a Wendy's Kids' Meal. I feel there was a photograph taken of this that I remember seeing, and I wonder if it still exists somewhere. I remember resting on the snake's head and I remember the photograph of myself resting on it equally. I liked this day, seeing these things that seemed so important, Dad mostly hanging back in the wet shade of the jungle edge, not climbing things. He had brought me here and I loved it. I felt the secret urge children have to become lost and stay overnight somewhere good, like a museum or mall, as a way of being there privately, directly. I circled the pyramid hoping to find a cave where I could curl up, so I could sleep and stay inside this old magic, like a good sacrifice, just right for something serious. But it was hot and we had to go. Dad seemed tired, suspicious of it all, not especially interested in learning too much from the guide or in looking too hard at the ruins. I was happy, though, and he was pleased with that. He seemed to want to let me have my happiness without necessarily sharing in it or talking about it. Perhaps it's easy to dismiss children's happinesses because they seem so uninformed.

On the way back, our tour van had to stop for gas. Children my age but much skinnier came to the windows with their hands out, pleading and keeping steady eye contact. Some tourists in the van gave them coins. The kids who received coins immediately pocketed them and outstretched their hands again, empty. I looked at my dad. He laughed dismissively. "They're just bums. They can work like the rest of us."

And then, back to the days like before, which now seemed even longer. I grew tired of the pretty beach. The tourists were loud, desperate in their drinking and blaring radios. I sat alone in the hotel room for a few days as the vacation shrunk to the end. The room was yellow and clean and there was a small TV I would flip through endlessly. I had done a poor job of having fun. My sister would have known, implicitly, what to do. She was *made* of beaches and loud radios and virgin strawberry daiquiris and laughing at Dad's jokes and hamming it up for his camera. I imagined her there in the room with me: her correct joy and acceptance of this neon fun. She would not have let me lie there in my bathing suit and watch TV in Cancun. She would have pulled me out of the hotel's corridors where I wandered aimlessly, cold hallways tiled brown, the smell of chlorine from the pool trapped forever both night and day. Without her I walked from the room through the hotel and back to the room again with the twenty-dollar bill he had given me for food, not sure what to do with it.

10

How is it that I am my father's daughter? Something feels fraudulent about our blood bond. Before my sister and I were born there was an irrevocable fraudulence Dad carried out against my mom, and I can't help but assign significance to this.

Dad steered Mom through the broad doors of the restaurant at the Hazel Park racetrack for their first date. The old host lit up, welcomed him by name, and seated them by the wide windows. The waiters knew him too, and he tipped outrageously. Mom wore a baggy white hippie smock embroidered with lines of tiny red flowers (a dress, she said, like "a loose interpretation of a baseball") and her wild, black curly hair down in a loose cloud. Dad wore a gold-button sports jacket, creased slacks, and hard-shined shoes, slick hair, a near Robert De Niro. They'd met while working in a tool-and-die shop in

Romeo, Michigan, in 1977. Mom had been placed there by a temp agency and had been working there only a few weeks.

After only a couple months of dating Dad took Mom on an elaborate vacation to South America to see Machu Picchu. He'd first suggested Mexico, but Mom said she didn't like Mexico. It made her nervous.

The trip was impulsive and strange, something my mom would have loved. And he seemed so rich. He'd told her, I imagine in his shy way, without eye contact, that if he ever were to marry someone, it would be her. Mom felt adored, scooped up in his big gestures, bound by the certainty of them. I have seen some of the photographs from this trip. They both look excited, free, and wild, in jeans and thin T-shirts, laughing, almost childish against the ancient monuments and green vistas. He directed this trip out of sheer confidence, ever calm, bullying through the language barrier, tossing my mom indulgences along the way, like the king of the parade.

"I didn't know," Mom tells me at the end of this story, "that he cashed in a life insurance policy to take me on this trip. He was dead broke. By the end of it he'd run out of money and we roamed Lima aimlessly, subsisting on street vendors' hot dogs and fruit he'd steal from the market stands."

I have to stop her. "Wait. Did you know he was stealing fruit? Were you stealing it with him? You must have realized he was broke?"

"No, I didn't know. He'd make me wait somewhere while he went to get lunch or dinner. I only realized later when I found out about the life insurance policy."

"And how did you find that out?"

"Oh, his wife told me when I met her."

His wife. Dad had a wife when he started dating Mom. We sit on the couch in silence for a moment with the facts. Dad in Peru stealing fruit from a stand like a child for his girlfriend, his wife and child hidden from her, the stealing hidden, *everything* hidden. For Mom there was only the fruit and the vacation and this fun man. What great lengths he'd gone to for her. The incredible energy expended in lying and hiding and stealing his own life insurance policy away from his family to give to my mom. He looks so relaxed in the photos. Not a trace of strain.

Soon after the trip she discovered she was pregnant with my sister.

Mom's pregnancy started to show at the tool-and-die shop, drawing hostile looks from the bitter receptionist with the beehive hairdo. Mom noticed the looks, and turned to her in the break room directly, as Mom would if something needed to be sorted out.

"Darlin'," the receptionist said before Mom even opened her mouth, "he didn't tell you he's married, did he."

Mom laughed but said nothing. The receptionist just clucked and shook her head in pity. Mom didn't like pity. She would have ignored it. How he told her he'd marry her if he was ever inclined to marry, it just didn't seem like something someone already married could come up with, not in good conscience. It was so sweet. He was *so* generous, so affectionate.

The idea began to itch her. She did think it was odd that she had never been to his house, didn't have his phone number, and had only vague indications of where he lived. That night she asked him plainly if he was married, and he said no. He acted genuinely confused by the question, suggesting that the receptionist was just a jealous cow because he wouldn't flirt with her. His answer was exactly right. She felt happy with that. And besides, there was a baby to consider now. She let it go. Soon, she moved into an apartment with him and quit working. My sister was coming to change things.

For her first doctor's visit, Dad gave her his insurance card and the name of the clinic to visit while he was at work. She handed over the card to the receptionist, who pulled a file, opened it, then paused. The receptionist looked at Mom, then to the file, then to Mom, and so on, glancing at the nurses near her to spread her discomfort around to them too. An indignant look hardened her face. Mom was puzzled. "Is everything OK?" she finally asked.

"Yes but . . . I'm sorry, ma'am . . . but you are not Mrs. Brodak."

Mom smiled politely. "Well, not officially yet, but I'm on his insurance now so you have to honor that . . ."

"No, I mean . . ." The nurses now looked on with worry. "Mrs. Brodak and her daughter are regular patients of this clinic. They were just in last Wednesday. *You* are not Mrs. Brodak."

It was then, she told me, that it should have ended. It wasn't too late. "Everything," she told me, "could have been avoided if I had just gone back to my parents instead of him the moment I left that clinic." I nod, imagining how much better that would have been for her, skipping past the idea that this "everything" she could have avoided would have included me. "It's like all I could do was make mistakes," she said.

She felt very small. This is a version of Mom I didn't know. She seemed so weak in this story, so fooled by him, that it starts to seem all a little unbelievable. Was Dad really this powerful? Or was Mom simply weaker then, a naïve child?

She turned and left the clinic as the nurses chattered in a sharp hush behind her. But maybe there was an error. Her thoughts turned to her baby.

The moment he stepped through the door that evening she told him the story of the insurance card at the clinic, and demanded to know who the real Mrs. Brodak was. He softened his shoulders and toddled gently to her, engulfing her with a hug and caressing her as she cried. His softness and confident denial stunned her into silence. He told her the woman was just a friend he'd let use his card, that he was just doing someone a favor out of kindness, and he was certainly not married. He laughed about it, prodding and rousing her into laughing with him as he smoothed her face.

He could turn you like that. He just wouldn't let your bad mood win. He'd steal your mad words and repeat them until they were funny, poke at your folded arms until they opened, grin mocking your pout until you smiled, as long as it took. He'd pull what you really wanted out of you—affection—and cover you with it until the offense was smothered out.

Thoughts began to itch her again, harsher now, when she was alone. Things seemed wrong. A few days later she called the county clerk's office to inquire about some marriage records. The clerk on the other end delivered the news plainly, as she probably always did. He'd been married for just a few years. He had a daughter, age four.

See, this is how my dad starts as my dad—stolen away from another family.

Mom packed her small suitcases and moved to her parents' house that same day, and that, again, should've been the end of it. She stayed in her room. The road to her parents' house north of Rochester, Michigan, had not been paved yet, and there were still fields surrounding them, overgrown lilac bushes, honeysuckle, wild rhubarb, where now there are neighbors' neat lawns.

She thought about his tenderness. Long periods of separation between their dates felt zipped shut by his total adoration when they were together. Honest, steady light in his eyes when he told her he loved her. He'd sweep her up for a small dance around the kitchen suddenly. All these things he'd practiced with his real wife. She gave birth to my sister, quietly.

But he wouldn't leave her alone. He found her there and would come whenever he could, tossing pebbles at her window in the night like a teen until her father chased him off, or leaving bouquets on the doorstep with long love letters. The bounty of his insistence must have been convincing: the dozens and dozens of roses, the gifts, jewelry, the long letters pleading for forgiveness, praising her virtues, promising to leave his wife, "and poetry," Mom said. "You should have seen the poetry he wrote to me. I almost wish I hadn't thrown it all away."

First she wanted to meet the real Mrs. Brodak. Mom looked up their number in the phone book, called to introduce herself, and extended an invitation to meet, which Mrs. Brodak accepted, stiffly.

It was a muggy summer. Dad's wife appeared at the screen door and stood without knocking. In a thick blue dress with her waist tied tightly, she said nothing when Mom opened the door. "Would you like to hold the baby?" Mom asked.

My sister was placed in her lap like a bomb. Nothing could be done but politely talk, with hard grief in their chests softening their voices. The real Mrs. Brodak was scared too. "How did you meet?" she asked Dad's wife.

They met in high school. After returning from Vietnam, he married her impulsively. She never had time to think, she said. Baby, work, no time to think. How life works: hurrying along through the tough moments until the hurrying hardens and fossilizes, then that becomes the past, all there was, the hurrying. She asked Mom what was going to happen now.

"Now," Mom said, "we leave Joe Brodak. We don't let our babies know him. He's not a good person." She leaned to her, with hands out. They lightly embraced and nodded, tearfully. Mom would have wanted to help Mrs. Brodak. Mom would not have been able to help.

Mom also, somehow, would have felt a little triumphant. She would have felt like she won him. Whatever there was to win. Mom wouldn't have wanted to quit like that, despite what she said to Mrs. Brodak. She had a baby now, and no real career prospects, having ditched her student teaching and not quite finished her certification after graduating with her BA in special education. Her parents looked on with reserved worry. After Dad's wife left, Mom joined them in the kitchen, where they had been listening to the exchange carefully. They sipped coffee, looked out at the birdfeeder. At a loss, her mother urged her to go back to him. "It is better to be married," she said. "You have to just deal with it."

She turned to him, resolved to trust him. Mom isn't sure exactly when he finally got divorced from his first wife; he only said it was "taken care of." With her daughter, my half-sister, the real Mrs. Brodak moved to California, where she died of cancer a couple of years later.

This looks bad, I know. I would not have made the choice to return to him, I think. Most people wouldn't. But what do any of us know.

In the basement of the Romeo courthouse my dad married my mom, with his sister, Helena, as a witness. The dress she wore, an off-white peasant dress with low shoulders and small pouf sleeves, I wore at ten years old as a hippie Halloween costume, ha.

She didn't tell me then it was her wedding dress, just said it was an old thing. Too shy in our new neighborhood to trick-or-treat, I stood like a grown-up at our door in the dress, baggy and so wide-necked it barely stayed on my shoulders, while I passed out candy to kids my age. The night ended fast when I leaned down obliviously in front of a group of boys to pick up a dropped single-wrap Twizzler, my whole bare front visible in the huge tent of dress, down to my day-of-the-week underwear. I didn't know those boys but now they knew me. I hurried through that fifth-grade year tacked with the nickname "Moundy."

I asked Mom what Dad wore at the wedding, since I had never seen any pictures. "One of those corny polo shirts he had," she laughed.

A small dinner party was held at a nearby golf course restaurant. Mom met her mother-in-law there, and many other Brodaks, who all regarded her warily, as a homewrecker.

Soon after the wedding, I was born, during a year of relative happiness in their relationship. Perhaps, my mom thought, their rocky start was over, and with some commitment to discarding the past, there would be no more problems. She threw her wild energy into this life now: these children, and him, *her* husband now. She enacted a vigorous and healthy routine: reading, games, walks to the park, dancing, art, and helping the elderly lady upstairs with her housework. She made a point of holding me as often as possible. She said I was an easy baby, calm, happy, affectionate. "You hardly ever cried," she told me. "It was easy to be with you. Your sister was harder. She was two when you were born, so that's a hard time to get a sister. She hated the affection you got. She'd steal your toys but you'd just busy yourself with your toes or whatever was there. You two didn't get along."

Still, she attended us with pure devotion. She baked homemade bread and wrote folk songs for us, singing them softly to us with her acoustic Gibson at bedtime. The songs were always minor key, lament-low, about horses and freedom and the ocean. In the dark, I'd cry sometimes in their hold, chilled in their sweetness.

I know this is not so uncommon, a man with a second family. If it ever does come up among friends or acquaintances, there is almost always someone who has experienced this or knows someone who has. It is a thing that happens. Men have affairs, and the affairs become relationships, marriages even, decades long. I know the affair starts just for some new fun, for sex, to be wanted again, some other need the man thinks could be fulfilled without having to fully or officially leave his wife. And then, I don't know, maybe he really loves the second woman, or the child that comes along, more children, more bonds. More devotion? More love? Is it possible to love two families at once? I don't believe, not even a little, that it is possible. Maybe his shame shapes this "solution"—to secretly keep both families, support both, out of an honest sense of guilt or duty. I think Dad was just too proud to admit he'd done anything wrong. He doesn't mention wrongdoings or apologize. I think he didn't want to back out of his affair with my mom because he couldn't figure a way out without looking diminished, in a position of *error*, a position he could not abide.

Dad was already in prison when Mom told me that we were the secret family. I was probably fourteen. We were sitting in a car, parked in a driveway, and it was dark. We were waiting to pick up my sister from somewhere. I had, without thinking, asked Mom how she'd met Dad, and all of this rushed out.

I stared straight ahead, at a garage door, trying to picture what she was describing. I was trying to imagine my dad being husband to another woman, dad to another girl. I imagined their house, what it might look like, how he would have joked with them as he did with us, how he would have lain calmly in front of another TV on another couch in another house. Mom was sad to tell me; I could hear it. I felt a pit deepening in me.

Mom is the only one of us who thinks for certain that Dad is a sociopath. On a recent visit to her house for the holidays, I told her I'd been corresponding with him, just to keep in touch and to keep a line open. I told her I didn't want anyone else to know that I was going to write about this because I knew no one thought I should, not even her. But, out of everyone, she would understand. She handed me a book: *The Psychopathic Mind*, by J. Reid Meloy, a little outdated, from off the shelf in the guest bedroom. "He has no conscience," she said. "He doesn't know guilt. He hates to be caught, for sure, but he doesn't feel bad if he doesn't get caught. He simply wants what he wants and perceives people as objects to help or hurt those goals. Be careful talking to him. He will manipulate you."

I would have to find out what I could about him anyway. And do it alone.

11

Mom threw away all of the letters and poetry Dad had sent her when she married her new husband in 2004. It stings to think about. I wish to God I could have read those things, but they were not for me. And I don't blame her.

I did see the letters, a long time ago. I was little, maybe seven or eight, when I stumbled upon a shoebox full of them. There were pages and pages of blue-lined notebook paper with Dad's loopy and fat cursive writing, or the harsh, slanted block letters he'd use—handwriting I recognized instantly. The words rattled on the pages with a mysterious grown-up intensity that pushed me away from them. I left the letters, but I did take something: a puzzling black-and-white portrait photograph of him that he had sent her. The background is pure white and the whiteness of his knit polo shirt disappears into it so that his head appears to be floating in whiteness, rooted only by the wide, heathered gray collar of his shirt. He is young and smiling broadly, openmouthed, joy in his eyes, as if he was just laughing, really laughing. He's smiling honestly, more honestly than I have ever seen.

On the back of the photo is his loopy cursive in blue pen:

```
Nora,
    My first real, true love. You changed my life
with your "crazy" love.
    I love you,
    J. B.
```

When I read these words I began to cry instantly, in gusting sheets of tears. I took the photograph because it was the first object that ever made me cry.

12

They say the traits of a sociopath are incessant, sometimes even pointless dishonesty, lack of impulse control, and lack of remorse, accompanied by charm, narcissism, and studied manipulation.

Skimming through the basic criteria for this personality disorder in the DSM-5 I was struck by how obviously this description suited my dad. I had to laugh a little.

So how can I still doubt it? Somehow I do. Maybe a person can just be a regular man with problems, who just keeps making increasingly bad choices to cope with the messes from old bad choices, over and over. Does it *have* to be that he is a sociopath?

Psychologists today describe disorders or pathologies with fuzzy borders, in more baggy categories than they used to be—spectrums, with a range of traits that may or may not present themselves in the sufferer, and with a wide range of intensities. This offers a more intelligent and nuanced view of psychopathology, and softens overly broad, black-or-white generalizations about the meaning of disordered actions, such as crimes or compulsions. But, it also, in a way, makes the categories of mental pathologies less meaningful—it puts everyone, in some way, on every spectrum.

Certainly Dad falls a little farther along on the spectrum than, I don't know, everyone else I know. He's not a murderer, not productively domineering enough to be one of those successful, greedy, and coldhearted CEO types, nor is he reckless enough to have earned any other criminal convictions before the robberies. He's just fundamentally dishonest. And I can't say that of anyone else I know.

Dishonesty is a deep taproot for a sociopath. It feeds the manipulative powers, obviously, and all the crimes stem from a kind of manipulation, *a falseness of being*, even to those closest to him, or especially those closest to him. Dishonesty is cumulative, building layers of masks upon the original self, useful for quick changes, for opportunistic shifts that cut straight to personal goals without the messy effort of considering others. Deceptive masks can become burdensome, exhausting. I hold out hope that he will drop his. I wouldn't still be thinking about him if I didn't believe there was something true under his lies.

But lack of remorse. That one is hard.

Dad shows remorse for his crimes, all the lying and stealing and cheating. I see it in the photo of him wearing his orange jumpsuit that pops up when I Google his name. It stabs me cold when I see it, and I have to look away. There is emotion in his eyes. But maybe it is just plain anger.

His letter to the sentencing judge at his last trial was, honestly, convincing. But it is hard to know what I'm looking at when I read it. He really does seem to deserve leniency, with his bold moral regret, acknowledgment of misaligned priorities, clear reasons for his fogged judgment. Perhaps this shows growth, a maturity that came with age and genuine reflection on the consequences of his poor choices.

But in a sociopath, what looks like maturity is often just a more sophisticated set of skills in manipulation.

What is the difference?

13

After I was born Dad came across an ad for an attorney who hired women to be surrogate mothers and he became convinced this would solve my family's financial problems. Nowadays paid surrogacy is more common, but at this time in the early eighties the process was new and still somewhat risky. He pressed upon my mom this idea, that this procedure could relieve them of their debt and provide a nice financial cushion for the family. She started to warm to the idea. After all, she loved being a mother, and the possibility of helping a couple have a baby felt kind and smart and wonderful. She said the couple met her in a restaurant, and she brought me and my sister along, "you know, to show you off, so they could see how healthy and happy you were," she told me. We squirmed and smiled in the booth like the best roly-poly babies possible, and Mom beamed while the couple fell for her.

The couple lived on Long Island, so Mom was flown out to New York to do the insemination there. It didn't work. She was flown out again. It didn't work.

Meanwhile, Dad's gambling debts were secretly accruing. He had started thinking about the $10,000 they were set to receive as soon as the baby was born, and he revved up his spending and reckless gambling. Mom didn't know about the gambling yet, but its effects were becoming obvious. The kind old woman who lived upstairs came down one evening to offer Mom some homemade bread and soup—a regular event, since the woman could see we didn't have quite enough food to go around. "Oh, and your brother-in-law was here this morning looking for you," she told Mom.

"Brother-in-law?" Mom asked. She did have a couple of brothers-in-law, but why would one come down to Auburn Hills?

"He seemed real nice, kept asking about you and the girls. Asked where the girls go to school now. He asked what they looked like too, how big they are now and all that."

Mom froze. She buckled over and begged the woman to say she hadn't told the man anything about her girls. The woman brought her fists to her mouth and began to cry lightly, realizing now that the man had not been a brother-in-law, stammering out that she had not told him much, had not known the name of the school we attended.

Mom recounted the scene to Dad once he arrived home. He laughed gently and said he was sure it was nothing. But then he fell serious. "Anyway," he instructed her, "ignore knocks at the door.

"On second thought," he corrected, "hide under the bed when someone knocks."

Mom carried on in this apartment in terror. The phone rang incessantly during the day when he was gone. Afraid to leave the receiver off the hook in case she needed to be reached, she hid it in the closet. Only once did she pick it up and respond to a strange man on the line. He told her he was calling from Vegas. "Your husband," the man said, "is a scumbag. A fucking deadbeat. Did you know that?" She unplugged the phone. That night, the living room windows were shot out.

It was Dad's ideal moment to convince her to move. She was afraid now, and tired of living off beans and handouts from the neighbors. Dad said he had a prospect of a better job—and it just so happened to be on Long Island, closer to the couple, how ideal.

We moved to a cramped basement apartment on Long Island. In photos of us from this era, atop a cheap swingset or feeding ducks by a weak pond, there is a kind of stressy child anger in our eyes. But Mom kept up her focus on us. Free from his debts back in Michigan, Dad returned to gambling. She never knew how bad things were until something turned up missing. A car, for example.

One morning, Mom was cleaning us up from breakfast as Dad was leaving for work. He came back into the house after a minute. "Forget something?" Mom asked absently.

"No, uh, my car . . ."

Mom looked out the window. It was gone. "Where's your car?"

"Oh . . . I let a buddy of mine borrow it."

"He just came in the night and took your car? He had a key to your car?"

"Yeah, it was an emergency, no big deal. I'm gonna borrow yours today, OK?" He grabbed her keys and left.

How could he resolve this one? Weeks went by and his "buddy" didn't return the car. Eventually he just came home with a new one, an old beater with green upholstery that smelled like dogs. He told Mom he'd just decided to sell his buddy the car, but she'd already seen the repo notice. She wasn't surprised anymore. She shuffled her rage into resignation, and focused on us instead.

The insemination attempts continued. One night, after returning from a long trip to a casino, drunk and tired, Dad forced himself on Mom. She said she screamed and fought him. But he was strong. Sex violated the contract they had with the couple, for obvious reasons.

On a hunch, she took a test a few weeks later and discovered she was pregnant. Now, though, she wasn't sure whose baby it was.

She felt totally lost. She took us to stay with her aunt in Baltimore for a few weeks. And there, without telling anyone, she decided to abort the fetus. She hadn't spoken to Dad for weeks, nor did she return the calls from the couple. Eventually she returned home, with us in tow, to find Dad having just returned too, from Atlantic City. He had gambled away everything; their savings, his car, his wedding ring, every penny he could find. Mom packed our clothes again and whatever small things would fit into her powder blue Caprice Classic, and took us back to Michigan that same day. She filed for divorce and moved back in with her parents, again. It was while living with my grandparents that I first started to know my life. I remember Goodison preschool. A salt-dough Christmas ornament I made there that I tried to eat. Playing red rover in the sun. My bossy sister teasing me, other young children around, and a stress around us all.

Eventually Mom was going to have to call the couple to tell them what happened. She says she still remembers that phone call, their voices on the other line, warm, but quiet and shocked. They were crushed. They said they would have taken the baby either way, and loved it completely. They had come to trust and care for her, and she failed them in the worst possible way. Listening to my mom reveal this story crumples my guts coldly.

14

My first memory happened on a stairwell, and stairwells have had special resonance as meaningful sites for me ever since. I was three years old, maybe. The stairs were wide and thin, the kind with no back to the steps, just floating slats. It was sunny and the room was white and yellow, the stairwell of an apartment building. Mom was ahead of me, on the steps above, holding paper bags of groceries in both arms. I fell. I was belly down on the steps, and I could see through to the emptiness behind and under us. I can see it now. Just a column of pure air. I was afraid I would slip through, into space, even though I wouldn't have fit through the slats. I looked up at Mom, who kept climbing the stairs strongly and calmly. "Get up," she said. "Come on."

15

Such a short part of their lives really, this marriage. Just a few years.

Dad moved back to Michigan too, following us a few weeks later. Now it was 1985. We had moved, on average, every year and a half and would continue this pattern until I hit middle school. Mom and my sister and I returned to Grandma and Grandpa's house. Dad was living in a hotel room in Centerline, near the GM Tech Center where he worked.

We would be dropped off there, and walk the Astroturf-lined hotel walkways to the room while teenagers screamed and splashed in the pool. Latin music blared and faded from within the rooms we passed, some with open doors, some with eyes following. It seemed like a party. Dad bought us huge bags of candy: Skittles for my sister, Raisinets for me. There were always cold cuts and a shrimp ring in the fridge. During the day he'd often leave us alone there, and we were OK, watching movies, eating candy, puffy painting giant, cheap sweatshirts and playing Nintendo—Super Mario Bros., Mega Man, and Rampage, all day.

My sister took care of me when we were alone. She directed me to eat from the plate of crackers and ham she'd arranged and to drink a glass of milk when I was too absorbed in a game to eat. She knew how to pull out the sofa bed when we were getting tired. I'd watch her tiny body rip the creaky metal frame out of the nubby brown couch like some industrial conjuring trick. She'd straighten the sheets around the lumpy mattress and drag the comforter from Dad's bed onto ours, nestling me into the uncomfortable mess wordlessly.

She'd check to make sure the front door was dead bolted, then flip the lights off and tuck us in. The puffy paints, bags of candy, half-consumed glasses of milk, and plates of ham would be scattered on the floor around the sofa bed, and we'd just lie there, listening. The rush of cars on 12 Mile Road below and the garbled living sounds from the residents in nearby rooms would lull us to sleep. We imagined different versions of where Dad was; a cool movie, on a date with a hot lady, at a nightclub, at a concert. Sometimes we'd compare ideas, sometimes we'd just let them play out in our heads as we fell asleep.

During the day I'd poke around his stuff when he was gone as I always did when I was left unattended. Shoved under towels in the linen closet were *Playboy* magazines and a few tiny baggies of green and white drugs. Sometimes money.

Under the bed, in a shoebox: a heavy, greasy-looking gun. Just once.

I didn't really miss him when he was gone, but I knew that couldn't be right. I wanted him around, but when he was I felt awkward near him.

I wanted to have the fun he wanted us to have. He'd take us to kid things, like water parks or Chuck E. Cheese, places Mom would never take us to because she insisted on productive activities, like hikes or art museums. Regularly he'd take us to a golf dome with a bar and a dark arcade attached, then hand us both a roll of quarters to spend in the arcade while he was in the bar. For hours we'd feed the machines, Mortal Kombat, Rampage, and Gauntlet. When our quarters were gone we'd gingerly shuffle through the bar and find him alone, glued to a sports game usually. He'd hand us more quarters or say it was time to go. It was fun, but thin fun. I felt lonely. He'd put something in front of us—a sports game, an arcade, a movie, or a toy—but he was always on the other side of it . . . far on the other side of it. I kept it that way too, I know. I didn't like to go with him. I didn't like to have to answer his perfunctory questions about school or interests. I didn't even like to hug him.

I see my little self standing awkwardly next to him. I had wanted to be hugged, for sure. I had wanted him to ask me questions. Maybe it's my own fault that I couldn't figure out how to love him like my sister did.

And once again, he pursued Mom relentlessly. I didn't know this until later, when Mom told me. I often wonder why he pursued her. He could have easily walked away from us, and perhaps he didn't only because that was the more obvious thing to do. The only thing that makes sense is that he wanted to be with us. Or, he felt like he was supposed to be with us, an obligation he couldn't shake.

I can't feel my way toward a sharper picture of him. Nothing really matches up. There are fragments of a criminal alongside fragments of a normal dad, and nothing overlaps, nothing eclipses the other, they're just there, next to each other. No narrative fits.

16

No, I did see it, once. On a softball field, in the evening, when the sky was turning dark pink. Mom had brought me to see my sister's after-school softball team play, a team that my dad coached. I had wandered away out of boredom to sit in the grass, probably looking for interesting insects or rocks, and from some distance I saw my dad approach my mom at the edge of the bleachers where she stood. The sun was behind them, but I could see their gray shapes in a nook of the gleaming silver bleachers and the matching fence. Perhaps the game was over. He was talking close to her face, and she was looking away at first, arms crossed. I edged to the other side of the bleachers to hear. He had his hand on her shoulder; she was starting to smile. I could hear him say, "I need you. I need you," in a steady, pleading voice that I can still hear in my head. I was surprised at this sound, and memorized it. Then he lifted his knee and softly and childishly kneed her thigh, still saying "I need you" and now drawing it out lightly and funnily with each jab, "I *kneed* you. I *kneed* you," and she was really smiling now, looking down sweetly and smiling.

17

And so it all started over. Mom and Dad were getting back together and I should have been happy. Mom should have been happy, but she wasn't.

Mom and my sister and I piled into the Caprice Classic and left Grandma's house in the fall of 1986, pulled by Dad's spell. Mom sobbed as she watched Grandma's house shrink in the rearview mirror. She turned her face away from us, but I saw her crying. I felt guilty. Even now I don't think Mom would have gone back to Dad if it weren't for us kids.

Dad rented half of an old duplex on Laurel Street in Royal Oak, then still a lower-working-class suburb before it gentrified in the late nineties. At Mom's request, Dad agreed to go to Gamblers Anonymous, but quit after a few sessions, just when, according to him, the group started to "pry" into him. "I'm not that bad," he told her. "These guys, they're crazy, I mean really stupid, how they gamble. I know what I'm doing."

Mom kept pushing him to go back, but he threw himself into working instead, picking up all available overtime at GM. Mom had finished her graduate program and was working steadily. We had a year on Laurel Street—and it was a big year for me. I was five years old, and my world was starting to solidify whole around me and become readable.

The duplex had an angled stairwell set in its center like a spine and a musty basement smell. On the middle landing of the stairwell there was a door that led nowhere, just outside, straight down. Mom told me that there was probably once a porch there; surely there must have been a porch there, although you couldn't see any evidence of it from outside. The dead bolt on the door was kept locked, but when I was bored I would quietly unlock it, turning the knob so slowly that no one would hear. I gently pulled the door open, hoping to quiet the sucking sound of it opening. I stood at the edge and looked down at the flat lawn. It was not high, not even on the second floor yet, but still it was terrifying. I loved that door. It made me feel like things could be insane and senseless in any regular home and it was just going to be like that; it was *built like that* in fact.

There is a photo of my sister and me sitting on the front steps of this duplex. We hold new kittens. My sister is looking right at the camera, delighted, and I am looking away. The kittens, Max and Shema, held some promise of normalcy. Surely we were home now; after all, we had kittens, and kittens required stability. But I am wincing, and somehow look already defeated. Like a nonbeliever already, at six years old. On the sidewalk in front of this house there is a ghost of me learning to ride my bike, Dad running alongside patiently, holding the handlebars and keeping me steady until I can balance. From then on, my bike was everything to me—my instrument of freedom and privacy. Then, there was the Bike Disaster, as Mom called it.

My sister was riding her bike and I was set upon Dad's handlebars because my bike had a flat tire. We were just going around the block. "Keep your feet real open," Dad had told me. My bare feet hovered away from either side of the whirring front wheel. It felt good to be charged with such a challenge. I was strong and I could do it, easily even. Dad sped up down the long block, and I looked back to see my sister charging fiercely to catch up, smiling and bright faced. Dad leaned into a corner and in went my foot. My ankle hit the blur of spokes and was chewed: Dad skidded to a stop, grabbing my body back to him, holding me up and away from the bike and bloody wheel. I did not scream at first, but marveled at the foamy spray of blood up my legs, confused.

Dad screamed. Someone from inside a house rushed out, an ambulance was called, a hospital was visited, and a cast was applied. I started the first grade with this cast on my leg, dirty after only a couple of days because I would not stay indoors. "My dad," I told anyone who asked how I ended up in the cast. I hardly understood what that implied.

Because the landlord intended to raise our rent the following year, my parents got married. Dad wanted to buy a house, but Mom wouldn't agree to it unless her name was on it too, so they got married, as a "business arrangement," Mom said. This house, on Bonnieview, the only real house I have ever lived in with my parents, was the "bad" house. Our family dissolved for good in that house.

My parents got married at the courthouse and had a reception in the basement. I remember them cutting a flat white cake together, both their hands on the knife. I remember Mom wore a vivid blue sweater tucked into a long, dark paisley skirt. Dad had a moustache then, and those big, square wire glasses mild office men wore in the eighties. I didn't understand why they were getting married.

In a Polaroid my mom sent me from the ceremony at the courthouse, the four of us are standing in front of a small group of trees. Mom is wearing a white jacket and a white skirt with a huge flower pinned to her shoulder. She has on an odd white hat and her big glasses, tinted pink at the top. My sister and I are glued together in front, huddled almost, in white frocks and squinty grins. Dad stands behind in a black suit. A real suit. Mom and sister and I form a kind of white pyramid against Dad's blackness. I stare hard at this photo. I have no memory of this event.

I loved the new house at first. It was the first proper house I had lived in with my family, and it was really ours, and we were really a family now. I had my own room, an incredible canopy bed with rainbow ruffles hanging down, and my own small, pink radio that I would hug like a doll as I fell asleep.

This was the time we were a normal family, for just a few years. Normal school, birthday parties, forts in the living room, our sweet cats, dinners together. Dad and Mom were putting on their "We're OK" hats and we girls did, too. I figured this was it: this was normal. For three years we all lived together. It seems absurd to imagine now, the four of us living together, like an impossible mirage.

I had no idea how not normal things were. But that's the thing about normalcy—it's only a frame of reference, not absolute.

Mom's hands shook while she washed the dishes, rattling silverware and splashing water onto the counter and up her arms. Some days she didn't leave her bedroom. The door would stay dark and silent all day, until I went to bed. Other days she'd take up some monumental project and leave it midway through, like the time I woke up on a Sunday to find one of my bedroom walls frantically half-painted dark blue, never to be finished. I didn't mention it. I just tried to be gentle around her, and began to realize that something was wrong with her.

I don't remember any childhood friends from this time, or any time really until I got to sixth grade. I wasn't interested in making friends. I didn't know what the point of friendship was, couldn't see any real value in it because I just wanted to be alone. And girls didn't seem to like me very much. I was confused by their interest in craftsy friendship bracelets and gymnastics and stickers and Lisa Frank junk. I wolfed down my lunches alone, then hurried to the library to avoid them.

During recess I sat near the recess monitors, watching the kids on the playground with the same distant interest as the adults did. Or I'd find a tree to sit under alone. I loved one crabapple tree high up on a grassy slope that became a snow-packed and dirty sledding hill in the winter. The sweet-rot vinegar smell of the fallen apples kept the other kids away, and attracted bees, which I loved to let crawl on my arms.

It didn't seem wise to get attached to anyone.

At home I mostly spent time alone outdoors. If she wasn't busy, Mom would sometimes join me, sunk into a squat lawn chair in the sun patch of our small backyard, eyes shut, a Bartles & Jaymes wine cooler in hand, her bathing suit straps down around her shoulders, exposing the smudgy, pastel star-and-moon tattoos on her chest. We didn't make small talk when we were together. We just rested.

I liked to dig. I wanted so badly to find something good. My sister's habit of pointlessly pulverizing rocks with a hammer into dust became a cleanup job for me. I'd found an old glass Coke bottle in the garage that I would fill with the dust. then sprinkle it out onto the things I cared about, my violets or the ladybugs I'd caught and kept in a small screen-and-pinewood box labeled THE BUG HUT.

I felt insignificant. I sought abstract things to confirm my insignificance, and still do: dirt, bugs, dust, geology, cells, the vastness of space, unpopulated places. Wherever no one was, I went.

All the way up to the roof. There was a small antenna tower right next to the house, touching it, hidden in the trees on the shady side of the house. It blocked the view from one of the windows in my room. It emerged from the dirt near where my private patch of violets grew and I toyed with climbing it one day. It was a Sunday and my sister was away playing with friends, my mom was resting, and Dad was gone. The tower was a little flimsy, didn't seem like it was meant to be climbed, but I decided it would hold me until I reached the roof. I made it to the warm black roof and sat, a little scared, the sharp sweet-and-salty smell of tar and sunshine all mine. I grew calm. I watched the other kids walking around the streets or in the adjacent backyards and I thought about the people in their cars and where they were going. I crept to the chimney and hugged it. I peered down into it: nothing to see but powdery black. A low weak whistle and a cool current of air jetted steadily upward from it. The treetops roiled in the wind. No one saw me.

After that I climbed onto the roof whenever no one was looking and stayed as long as I could, into night even. Sometimes I'd even see Mom come out and yell absently for me, toward the streets, not imagining I was above her. I liked to see her, and the whole world, small like that.

Toward the end of this three-year period, I started to notice how much Dad yelled at the TV. It woke me up. After bedtime I'd sneak down the hall to look at him in the living room, watching a basketball game in the dark blue light, sometimes two TVs set up side-by-side with different games during the playoffs, him yelling, holding papers, pencils, making calls. I had no clue he was gambling, or any notion at all that this was what gambling looked like. The yelling just seemed rude. And the louder he became the quieter I became. Some nights I'd creep out of my room to see about the yelling; once I cut my foot on a loose nail in the hallway and tracked blood back to my room but didn't tell anyone. In the morning, Dad was furious about the blood prints on the floor, and I knew his anger was not over the mess but the fact that someone had been watching him.

Soon there was constant fighting. The more they fought, the more the house faded. The fighting became the new house. I could feel the anger in my gut, even when there was silence, like a black hand threaded through me.

Then the old house seemed stupid, there in the background, like an obnoxious cartoon come on at the wrong moment. I used to love it. The wide flat sectional in the living room and its huge, flat-striped pillow my sister and dad would share watching the Lions on Monday nights, the brass-and-glass coffee table where I first saw Dad's squashed feet propped up (he told me he wore shoes that were too small as a child), the big TV, the dinette set with lacy woven cane seats that printed octagons on our thighs in the summer, and all of the rest: the cracked patio, the garage, the grass, the elms with white-painted bottoms like tube socks on big legs. It made me mad, how nice all of it was. It didn't seem to matter anymore; it wasn't us anymore.

One dim summer evening I found my mom crying alone on the front patio. I sat beside her on the concrete step and hugged my knees, just like she was doing. I didn't want to look at her. She just cried, straight ahead, into the cool night. She tilted and hugged me. I said, "It's OK, Mom, things are going to be OK, really . . ." which made her cry harder, waves of full body sobs. I decided not to cry, and in not crying, I felt old for the first time. I pushed myself down, out of love. The pushing created a pit, a blank resolve, to never make more pain for anyone. That resolve is still there somewhere.

Now I was eight years old. At the start of the new school year Mom insisted I go to a counselor at my school for an hour a week. The counselor told me what to do when my parents fought: go to your bedroom, put a pillow over your head or crank up your music and try to ignore it. This was the exact opposite of what I would do when they fought. Her suggestions seemed bizarre and sad. When my parents fought I would sneak toward the fight, hiding close to it so that I could hear what was being said. Most of it made no sense. I couldn't make out the words; it was as if it wasn't even English. There were yelps and repeated syllables and gravelly swear words and the most horrifying element of all: Dad's laughter, attempting to lighten the mood. I went toward it because I wanted to know what was happening, and because I wanted to hear my parents talking to each other.

I told the counselor that I cranked up my music when they fought. I'm certain I never told the counselor anything real about my life. She was warm and patient with me, and seemed genuinely interested in helping, which made me distrust her more fiercely than any adult I had met before. When asked to draw a picture of a favorite family memory, I drew all of us caroling in the snow at Christmastime, which she cooed over and urged me to cherish as a sacred memory I could access whenever I was sad. Nothing even remotely close to this ever actually happened. I had never been caroling, only seen it on TV. I just wanted her to leave me alone.

I remember clearly how it felt to be treated like a child. It made me feel deficient, like there was some weakness about me that forced adults to hide most honest or real things from me for fear of their effects. I didn't want that. I didn't want to be a child. It's underappreciated, I think, how quickly children can come to understand how to deal with adults in order to survive. I could see my parents' self-absorption. I knew they were hiding huge portions of their lives from me and all it did for me was to teach me not to trust them. And it ended our family. Never again would we live together in one house. I can't even recall a time since then when we all stood together in the same room, even for a moment.

One afternoon, my sister and I were playing separately, her making shooting noises with her G.I. Joes and me building Lego homes for my two precious My Little Ponys. My parents asked us to come have a talk in their bedroom. The room was electrified with tension. My sister and I sank into the puffy white comforter on the edge of their bed, sick-feeling, both of us, our faces mirroring each other.

They stood above us. "We are getting a divorce," Dad said.

Mom gave us a worried look. "I'm so sorry, girls. You know we love you very much and this is not your fault in any way." But we were too old for that line. Of course we knew it was not our fault; we had never considered such an insane suggestion until she'd said it. The idea of a divorce seemed fine, right even. I almost said "good" but held my tongue.

"Your mother cheated on me. Do you know what that means?" He spoke slowly and loudly, as if he wanted to hurt us with the words: "It means she let another man stick his penis inside of her."

I slumped as if cowering, went hot with tears. I felt sick from these people, how they acted and talked, the things they wanted, their stupid bitterness and coarse desires, how we had to be carried around recklessly by them.

"God fucking damn it Joe!" Mom screamed and he made an evil laugh. Mom began to cry and he just folded his arms. They began arguing blindly and we ran off, my sister to her room, and me to the little weedy plot on the side of the house, my garden, where I would talk to the wild violets as if they were my students. But that evening I stayed quiet, plucking the little rolled-up petals out of clover flowers and biting the tender white ends off, sometimes tasting the drops of nectar they were filled with, unless something had gotten there first.

18

Robins—the aimless tangled notes of robins in the morning—I awake to for years after their announcement. I can still hear my parents' voices. The sound of robins reminds me of somewhere we must have lived. I try hard to remember where. It must have been somewhere quiet—maybe when we went to live with my grandparents until I was about twelve. My space, the adjacent emptiness, a plot of harsh grass and Queen Anne's Lace, where I buried a time capsule I wanted to send to the future, filled, I don't know why, with broken mirrors and plates.

I can't place it. It's a spring feeling, one that can come too early, in January even, now that I live in the South. I spread flat the whole past and I'm not there. I see her, that little clueless me, but it isn't me. I don't feel scared or wistful looking back across this break in self, just grateful, honestly.

But aloneness is a thick curtain that gets harder to part. Far from my family, living alone, as I had always wanted I suppose, I would find it very silent in my small apartment most of the time.

19

"Dad?"

"Hey! Kiddo!" His whole self shook upward a little, startled. I walked too quietly and would just surface like that out of his blind spot.

"What is that?" I asked, and pointed to an embroidered patch tacked to the wall of the garage at the Bonnieview house, the bad one, the last one. Stitched in red thread against a black and yellow background were the words "I Know I'm Going to Heaven" (then some long chunky lump I couldn't recognize) "Because I Already Been to Hell" (then some abbreviations and numbers). The patch was telling me something about my dad so I studied it: it said that Dad had been to Hell, this scythe-shaped country outlined in red. It hung there as the only weird thing in the garage, like a crazy artificial flower above rows and boxes and drawers of tools laid straight and boring gray, functional items categorized by shape and size.

He laughed shortly, in a mean spirit, and set down the small parts he'd been messing with. "It's a patch from my old jacket," he said in his dumb kid voice, which was different from his adult voice, and I hated it for that reason. "After high school I got *drafted,* to the Army," then his voice turned brighter, "I had to go kill the yellow man," he said with an extra breathy rush of air.

"The yellow man?"

I took this to mean they wore yellow uniforms, like you'd call "shirts" the kids on the team wearing shirts and "skins" the half-naked ones. I imagined a whole army of men wearing yellow jumpsuits, and with no other useful information to construct their appearance, they all wore my dad's face.

"Yeah, chinks, you know," and he leaned down to me and pulled the corners of his eyes back with each pointer finger and made a comic grin. I smiled and pretended that this inscrutable gesture cleared things up, nodding. "See that too?" he continued.

Under the patch, propped straight into the corner of the garage where I had not looked before, was a long and narrow dagger.

"My bayonet! If you were real close you'd just ram it right into the little yellow men," he said, smiling and miming a jab. I couldn't tell if he was kidding. I watched his eyes. He was being funny, but with a bright hardness that was beyond me. I wanted to laugh but I didn't know why.

"Oh, cool."

20

I didn't know that the rest of the world didn't live intensely bound in a symbiotic net of relations with cars until I moved away from Detroit. Cars seemed as important as food, and my dad and all the other kids' dads were farmers. When he didn't work at GM he worked at a tool-and-die shop making auto parts, along with my mom. And if you didn't make car parts or assemble them you worked as a waitress near a plant, as I did as a teenager, serving workers on their lunch breaks. Ford, GM, Chrysler: God, Holy Spirit, Christ. We lived at their feet. That world, a web with the auto industry at its center, had been falling apart, and my family still lived in this falling-apart world. I grew up in a place that bled jobs and promises and no one really believed the bleeding would stop.

Desperation is not any one kind of thing—except maybe a mood. It's a mood people live in, and if you live in a Nice

Place, with clean parks and working streetlights and no hunger on your street, you only know this mood when you drive through the part of town you wish you could avoid.

It manifests in little habits for everyone, just small bad ways of being. Because things are Bad, and it soaks into everything and everyone. Would Dad have stolen if things were good? It's a big question, I know. Dad stole car things. He stole parts and materials from work; he eventually stole a whole car. The bank robberies could be traced back to, perhaps set off by, that car. A red Corvette convertible. A present for my sister.

We pulled up behind a small auto shop one evening when I was little, maybe six years old. I watched my dad get out of the car, climb a tall fence, and hop down into a pen of tires. He hauled one tire over the fence, then another, and put them in the trunk. When he came back to sit in the driver's seat he said, "They were fixing my tires. Didn't know they'd be closed so early." Watching him steal the tires, I was watching a secret. I felt more shock at hearing him acknowledge the action out loud, even with a lie, than at watching the act itself. I felt frozen and old. But his confidence, in this smooth, calm act of stealing—without hesitation, doubt, guilt, or whatever it is that would stop a person from stealing in front of his daughter—was almost a comfort.

21

In 2013 Detroit declared bankruptcy—the largest municipal bankruptcy in all of American history. People wanted to know how it happened. It frightened them. And it was weird and painful to hear people talk about it, especially at this distance. News analysts and reporters and politicians were wagging fingers with smug charges of everything from poor city planning to ruinous liberal unions to plain laziness. The story of Detroit's decline is trotted out as a cautionary tale, a story that flattens over what it's like to love Detroit as a home, an impossible home, one called the "Paris of the West" in the late forties. Yes, Detroit has been half-emptied by a long churn of riots, corruption, and the death of American auto manufacturing. The promised renaissance is always just around the corner, always coming but never arriving. My relatives and friends now live on the outskirts, places orbiting a black hole. And I abandoned it and all the rest of my family there, for Atlanta, a city that really did rise again after being burned to the ground during the Civil War, a city whose seal I see imprinted on the trash bins I pass on my morning run, a seal that lays bare a phoenix, face on, rising from a bank of flames toward the word *RESURGENS* above.

22

A year or two after my trip to Cancun with my dad, when I was eleven, I was sent to an Amish farm in Pennsylvania for the summer. It was sort of a camp, with other kids and preteens there too, about twenty-five of us in all, ranging in age from seven to twelve. It seemed clear from the way it was presented that it was a place for troubled kids. Since I knew I didn't *cause* trouble to anyone, I supposed, then, that I *was* the trouble that needed to be removed. After the second divorce, I was back at my grandparents' house with Mom and no sense of what might come next. I'm sure I seemed depressed and withdrawn at age eleven. I imagine Mom was eager for a chance to set me down into any wholesome world for a while. Certainly it was a respite. But I was not prepared for the virtue of that environment to illuminate my social dysfunctions so starkly.

It was sort of expensive—Mom told me that Grandma and Grandpa paid for it—so the kinds of kids there were mostly bratty rich kids whose parents wanted them to get to know something genuine, to experience hard physical work, and to appreciate "honest" living. There was a mom and a dad whom we were supposed to call The Mom and The Dad, but I refused. There were also several teenage children on the farm, along with pigs, goats, chickens, a few horses, a lot of cats and dogs, other small utility animals, and some scattered peacocks that seemed to have no purpose.

Upon arrival we were all issued straw hats and then handed newspapers and small buckets of diluted vinegar and told to wash the house windows. It was supposed to be some kind of brutal initiation but I was happy to have a task right away. I left my mom without hugging her, strongly reiterating my request for her to have Sun Chips with her when she returned to pick me up, and Guns N' Roses' *Appetite for Destruction* in the tape deck.

I loved the farm. It was set upon a hill and had wide views in every direction of pasture or farmland, and it was so quiet. Nights were windy and thick black on the hill. We slept in hard bunks, took cold military-style showers, and met in the barn before dawn to plan our work schedule for the day. A huge chalkboard stood near the mouth of the barn door, and The Dad would list the chores to be done that day, for which we had to volunteer. The chalkboard seemed as giant as a billboard and just as out of place in a barn. The Dad kept his one piece of chalk in his shirt pocket; I noticed only because I wanted the chalk so bad so I could write on the board. Without paper or pencils for weeks—even they had been confiscated on arrival—I ached to draw or write. In the downtime I'd sometimes sneak into the barn and trace words in cursive on the board with just my fingertip through the dust buildup. My favorite word to write in cursive was *eggs*. I loved the symmetry of the loops, and would trace it over and over, making each loop knot more perfect. Even now I catch myself repeating it in tiny cursive on grocery lists: *eggs eggs eggs*.

I always chose the hardest or most solitary work: grinding corn, milking goats, moving hay, tilling, chopping firewood. Most of the girls and the younger kids would choose the easiest stuff first—feeding animals, cooking, or cleaning indoors. I knew very well this was supposed to all be a kind of suffering for us. Work-wise, I could not be broken; there was nothing to break. I attached to my labor with a kind of mindless and helpless dedication children have when they throw themselves into something because there is simply nothing to lose.

After lunch we had "siesta time" for two hours. Most kids slept, out of real exhaustion, but I liked to do small private things I didn't have time for during working hours. My first choice was to collect eggs—not a real chore unto itself because the eggs came intermittently. I learned to distract the hen with a piece of hay while my other hand dove for her egg. I liked that the hens fought me and made an angry whine when I entered the henhouse. The back of my hand slid under their smooth bellies and I'd grab the egg carefully, sometimes accidentally clasping their horrible bony legs. Sometimes hens would bury their eggs in the hay troughs in the cool, dark goat barn. I'd dig through gingerly and find them, taking the discoveries to the house to The Mom, who was eternally busy with cooking or directing older girls as they cleaned.

Sometimes I'd just go into the granary shed and grind extra corn by myself. The roof was corrugated green plastic so everything inside was lit hot-grass green. The dried corn powder smelled warm and sweet as I cranked the grinder without thinking, in a thick fog of feeling. Work felt pure and right. I let it overtake every secret or lazy recess in my body. I wanted to see how good it could make me so I followed it all the way. It offered what I had been missing at home: structure, expectations, trust. The chance to *show myself* as a useful person. I discovered I loved to work. I wanted to be alone, so I wouldn't have to talk and break the feeling, or pretend to not feel it in front of others.

My challenge was not the work. At night, after all the work, dinner, and cleaning was completed, we had a little free time again before bedtime, in the living room. Free time, compared to work, became painful for me. In this restful and idyllic place, there was a fire, and a basket full of wooden toys, marbles, and puzzles. There was the Bible, or stacks of the Amish newspaper we could read by the oil lamps. And worst of all, there was The Dad, in his rocking chair, talking or reading a story. The littler kids clustered around him on the plain braided rug in different stages of exhaustion and stupor. The Dad was tall and wiry, with a neat beard and a straw hat—exactly as you are imagining.

Not having many friends in my life, I hadn't known other kids' dads. So after dinner, I'd sit by myself playing Shoot the Moon or completing a puzzle, and watch The Dad occasionally. The other kids grouped up into friendships and cliques, chatting about TV, music, or school—things I had instantly forgotten about upon arrival at camp. They weren't afraid to ask The Dad questions. I wanted to ask him questions but not in front of the other kids. And he was never alone. Mostly I just wanted to talk to The Dad, to have him hear me and to listen to him say what I imagined would be intensely wise things. I could see that this was what dads were for. The other kids seemed to know this, naturally. But I stayed where I was, watching the kids talk to him and feeling both jealous and annoyed with what they said; often they'd make jokes, asking him if he had heard of MTV or ever eaten at Burger King, never done being delighted with shock that The Dad had never experienced any of the dumb things central to their limited lives. He played along, and let the small kids crawl into his lap. Here was my chance to interact with a real dad, and all I could do was sit and stare.

Back on the first day we'd arrived, The Dad told us there would be two events we had to look forward to: the animal auction and the creek walk. It was nearing the midpoint of summer and the auction was approaching. Kids craved a break from the work routines and chattered about the upcoming auction at night. Then one morning, gathered in the barn, The Dad led us off the farm for the first time, walking together on a scorching, dusty dirt road to the livestock auction house. It was far and the walking was tiresome. High road cuts through the old hills, revealing roots and striations of mud, and some horses or cows near their fences were the only things to notice. Occasionally a horse and buggy came by, and even less frequently a car, for which The Dad would cover his mouth and nose to block the dust cloud it raised as it passed. This gesture also looked like a sign of disgust, and most of the kids copied the move, so it looked like the group was choking back puke or blocking a sick smell. I was up ahead a little bit and looked back to see them like that, The Dad and all the little kids like a gaggle of geese, and felt for the first time like there was something cultish about family, something dangerous. Somehow it could reduce you. I felt myself giving up a little then. I hadn't bonded with them or The Dad or anyone, as much as I wanted to. I was old enough then to start to wonder if there was something wrong with me.

We shuffled through the auction hall quickly, staying only a few minutes in the main auction arena, winding through the halls lined with animals in cages, then we turned to walk back to the farm.

At least the evening was cool in shadows and dusk light. I kept myself with the group this time. They started to sing, and I sang with them, looking down or straight ahead. The sky turned violet and pink and our voices seemed too loud among the empty hills. I imagined splitting from the group and running away for good. Then I thought about my mom. *Why can't I just join along and be happy*, I wondered.

The rest of the summer on the farm went on slow and weird. I wanted the work to be difficult for me, but it wasn't.

It was the other thing, the single point of comfort the other children clung to—The Mom and The Dad and each other—I couldn't manage. It had become clear to me I was broken. And then, about a month and a half into the summer, I got my period.

It wasn't the first one, actually; I had gotten my first period just before coming to the farm, uneventfully in the bathroom of a Red Lobster, but afterward I forgot all about it and didn't prepare myself at all for the idea that it would come back. I hadn't even told my mom the first time—just taken some of her pads in private and managed it myself so as to not bother her.

In the outhouse by the barn I stuffed my underwear with toilet paper and returned to my chore, chopping kindling. I could feel my toilet paper padding getting soggy. My stomach knotted.

I hurried into the house and found The Mom in the kitchen. She was standing on a chair, taking down a strip of stinking insect-studded flypaper to replace with a new one. "Ma'am? I got my period."

She stood on the chair, towering above me, her plump stomach bulging at the waistband of her long skirt, holding the long tongue of yellowed flypaper at my eye level. Her stern, unchanging face suddenly softened, and she seemed totally different. "Good, Molly, good for you."

She took me to her private bathroom upstairs and handed me a stack of pads. Not some kind of special homemade Amish pads, as I was sort of expecting, just normal Kotex Maxi

Pads. The overnight kind, thick as a diaper. I took them to my bunk bed and stuffed them into my pillow quickly before anyone could see me. I didn't want to be bothered with this new hindrance. I went back to work, feeling self-conscious about the pad's bulge and its awkward contact. I wanted to stop thinking about it and do my work like before, but I couldn't.

The next day, as we walked from the house to the barn in the cold dark morning, The Mom called after me. It seemed like she was unable to leave the house, only calling out for people if she needed something. I went back. I thought maybe she was going to check up on me, maybe give me some advice. "You will stay here and work with me now," she said, grasping my shoulders and smiling fakely. I nodded, and followed her to the first chore.

Then everything changed. I could do only housework with The Mom and the teen sisters, and the joy I'd just discovered in work was stripped from my days. Instead of going to the barn in the dark morning I washed dishes in the lamp-lit kitchen, soaked with the smell of flypaper and vinegar. I washed clothes on a metal washboard, scrubbing the shirts and socks of the Family as hard as I could. Then back to the kitchen for lunch preparation with The Mom and the sisters, who said nothing as they worked. At least there was silence. Sometimes a small kid would come to the kitchen with an egg or two she'd found in the goat barn and I really felt sad, holding the warm egg, locked inside.

After more dishes and cleaning, I'd iron with The Mom. Without electricity, of course, the iron had to be set onto the hot stove and then transferred quickly to The Dad's shirt on the board; his shirts were the only articles of clothing we ironed. He had a dozen plain white button-down shirts, which he wore no matter what kind of work he was doing on the farm. The iron had a wooden handle with two metal posts at the ends that would get hot and burn my hand if it wasn't held precisely in the middle. The iron was enormously heavy and had an evil presence. I hated ironing and I hated the The Dad's shirts. The first time I was assigned to iron it became apparent to The Mom that I had never ironed before and she showed her sharp disgust with me by frowning hard and drawing her eyebrows together but saying nothing as I struggled.

Now when I saw The Dad, I thought about smoothing his hot, clean shirt with my small hand after ironing it, and the weight of the iron, and the burns on my knuckles and palms, and the perfect flat brightness of his white shirt in the sun, chalk in pocket.

By the time the last event of summer came, the creek walk, I was too thin and fogged over in dreaminess to care about it. Being kept in the house made me feel sealed up, distant from the focus pure labor had first given me. It was hot and numbing in the house and the work didn't reach into me. Unlike The Dad, who left us to do our chores, The Mom watched me carefully in everything I did, ruining my private feelings most of the time. She couldn't catch me messing up or cutting corners because I didn't, not even when alone. I came to hate The Mom and The Dad's steadiness, the hardworking and loyal kids, even the obedient animals, all good cogs in the family machine—my simple childish jealousy of a healthy family crystallized into resentment.

And suddenly it was over. The last day on the farm we ate our breakfast of eggs and toast and apples in the cold dark with more silence than usual. We didn't have to work that day; we only had to pack and wait with The Dad on the lawn for our parents to arrive while the rest of the Family went on with the chores. Cars pulled into the driveway, and kids ran to them on sight one by one. My mom pulled up in her powder blue Caprice Classic and I ran to it too, saying goodbye to no one. I didn't look back, didn't want to see The Dad one last time. In the car, Mom hugged me hard and petted my hair, looking with some concern at my deeply tanned face and wild limbs. She pulled a bag of Sun Chips from the back and showed me the Guns N' Roses tape I had requested. I tore into the bag and slid the tape in. The chips tasted insanely potent, frightening, and the music sounded mean compared to the quietude of the farm. I turned it way down and smiled for her.

23

I don't want to see these words touching these true things. They are all wrong. This whole language I'm using is wrong. Language itself seems to fall to pieces when it touches certain topics. This is demon number one in this book.

But of course, here I am, already wrestling with demon number one, almost as if I couldn't help it. Nearby, demon two: storytelling.

Stories aren't helpful, are they? There is a reality—this one sliver of universe I'm assigned to—then there are the stories about it, working to "make" sense of it. Stories give Form and Meaning to our formless, meaningless stumbling through time. In stories our minds link, emotional survival techniques are transmitted, moral models are codified, hows and whys are satisfied. I know. But, then, is the story a kind of currency? Narratives are *bought* by readers and . . . what is sold?

Growing up as a voracious reader I found stories of pain and redemption on every library shelf I visited. Pain! Apparently pain, I learned, can be traded in. It is some kind of *money*, in these stories, traded in for love, or admiration, or credibility, or wisdom. In books and movies and poems and plays, this sort of redemption is only fair to the reader, after all, who is forced to endure along with the hero or sufferer. Sufferers *deserve* rewards. And it's so reassuring, the story of redemption.

Isn't it true?

Maybe it doesn't matter if it's true, because the alternative is simply too cruel to accept: that trauma is worthless. Grief has no meaning, it just is. Perhaps we have gained nothing from the psychological rending our dad enacted on my family. What if we aren't stronger or wiser, just hurt: the end.

I cringe at the word *deserve*. I just don't believe in deservingness. It stands a little too close to entitlement for me, uncomfortably close.

And if that's true, maybe there's an even better joy than redemption in knowing that pain isn't currency. It can be discarded! Maybe it isn't a raft, it isn't an identity, it isn't some grand cosmic test, it isn't shit.

Possibly. But could this line of thinking really *work*? After all, often it is this single point of comfort a sufferer clings to in order to endure: it will all be worth it on the other side, if I can just hang on—there's some love out there, some comfort, some wisdom. Others have earned these treasures after periods of suffering, according to these helpful narratives on the library shelves. This view of pain also demands fealty from other sufferers to ensure cohesion, I suppose, in regarding pain's purpose: the instructions from counselors and therapists to regard myself as *better* than before because of my experiences, "forged in the fire," they would say.

No stories work for me. The "story" I have felt these facts through is just a simple and untranslatable darkness. A packed wet powder, dark navy blue, nothing I could fit in a rectangular package and place on a library shelf. If I move or just look too closely I am afraid this "story" will crumble. This is one reason I never wrote directly about these true things. The other reason is that I thought they would not be meaningful to anyone, not even me, in any imaginable way.

Interesting, possibly, these things are interesting. But meaningful? *Who would care about my life?* It's a question, I realize, that's borne out of a framework of quiet childhood neglect, the kind that threads *no one cares* through a child's soft skull until it glazes over every little brain spark and network. Demon three.

Recently I was given a coupon for a session with a psychic astrologer, a session I attended with the sort of bemused skepticism I imagine most people feel toward these kinds of mystics. I entered the woman's loft just as her previous client was leaving, a soccer-mom type whose face I searched for emotional information about the effectiveness of the session: Was she crying? Disappointed? Did she seem pleased? She seemed pleased, pulling on her coat and rushing off. The place was clean and normal, like any office, and the astrologer greeted me as if I had come for a job interview. I sat before the astrologer, attentively taking notes as she read my chart quickly and occasionally interjected comments and advice "they" were telling her.

"You're a musician?" she said.

"Well, poet." Not a good start. But not painfully wrong . . . in the right ballpark at least.

"Oh yes, I see. Musician of words. The soundless music. Good. You're working on a book of poems . . . very good . . . keep going with that, it will be published in the fall." I nodded. Incredibly unlikely. Maybe she was just trying to encourage me, in the regular, nonmystical way.

"You're working on something else, too?" she said as if it had come to her suddenly. "Not poetry. A real book?"

A real book. Perfect way to insult a poet, but OK, I bit. "Yes, I'm working on a memoir of sorts."

"Yes. Now, listen to me." She pointed her open palms at me and spoke slowly. I held my breath.

"This *is* helpful to people, to write this. I can see you think it isn't."

My stomach dropped.

"But, listen. Everyone is in pain. You know this, I can see, you know you are not alone. Not everyone, though, not everyone knows this."

I instantly teared up.

"But you have to say it all. The raw part especially. That is the most helpful. The raw part."

The raw part. She'd seen right into my whole house, un-locked the basement, and pulled out the bit I thought I had hidden, and there she was, smiling blandly at me, holding it up, eyes saying, *Oh this, this raw part you put away, this is what you really need. And you know it, too.*

24

Fourteen-year-old girls stood with legs wide, humping the air or throbbing their butts at an imagined person, my sister at the center of them, wearing neon-rimmed sunglasses and a plastic BIRTHDAY GIRL tiara. She and her friends wore MC Hammer pants, the dump-crotch type, with skinny tank tops or boxy Hypercolor shirts. Jenny, the Korean girl with the masculine voice, and Kim, the girl with the worst red curly hair and white overalls with one shoulder undone, were whooping and pointing at my sister. There were about ten of them, in the crappy apartment building "clubhouse" Dad had rented for the night next to the molester-haunted pool. Never before or after would she have such an extravagant birthday party. Ghosty streamers bulged from the ceiling and the popular radio station blared from a tinny boombox. Open bags of Doritos sat gaping on tables. I sat on a chair, sort of watching the dancing, embarrassed, reaching into a Doritos bag occasionally. A honking car was approaching.

We all leaned toward the window, then screams rose, then the girls pushed outside. A shiny black stretch limo glided up before us, Dad towering out of the sunroof, arms spread, smiling and gnawing gum. The girls were losing their minds, hopping around with arms up, screeching in each other's faces. The car halted and Dad reached into his shining red Cardinals jacket pocket, withdrew a bank envelope, and threw it to my sister. The girls drew into a tighter frenzied circle around her, screaming now at the envelope in her clutches. I stood on the steps, wiping electric orange cheese dust on my bike shorts and giant flowered blouse. My sister unsealed the envelope and held up a stack of twenties for all to see. She began bouncing, and the girls held each other and bounced with her, yelling now. My sister waggled the bills in all of their faces. They began butt dancing again and hopping, hearing the music now, Kris Kross demanding jumps.

Dad ducked back into the limo, then emerged, opening the door for the girls to pile in.

My sister hesitated. "Is *she* coming with us?" she said to Dad, pointing with her nose at me.

The girls hunched and waddled in, hands on each other's backs, pushing. My sister and Dad stood, regarding me for a second, the orange smears on my bike shorts, my very un-fun face staring plainly.

Dad winced. Then smiled softly, fakely. "Yes. Yeassssss! Of course your sister is coming! You will look out for your little seester!"

My sister's chest caved in and she groaned. The girls were yelping for her to get in, absolutely incapable of waiting one more moment to arrive at the Four Bears Water Park teen club in this very limo. They were chanting something from the belly of the limo, straight white teeth and gel-crusted hair glinting blue behind the tinted windows.

I looked at the girls, and my sister. "I'm tired," I said. "I have homework anyway."

My sister popped up. "SEE. She doesn't even *want* to go. She's going to do her *homework*. LET'S GO!" My sister disappeared into the dark limo. Dad walked over to me with a pained expression.

"You sure? You want to go home? I'll walk you back."

"It's OK. It's right there. Bye Dad!" I limply hugged his waist and turned to the sidewalk back to our building. It was dark now, and I could hear them screaming along to some song I didn't know, and I was relieved, and they were relieved.

25

A photo of my sister that Mom sent me, which I had never seen before, frames her from a downward angle, most likely from Dad's hands. She's wearing his giant red satiny Cardinals jacket, half-swallowed in it, with his aviator sunglasses on and her feet in his huge brown loafers. She's frowning goofily, with some kind of small cigar plugged in the corner of her mouth. I don't recognize where she is; I don't recognize her at all from this time.

My sister and I divorced, just like our parents did.

I was nine and she was eleven when they got divorced for the second time, and Dad fought for custody of my sister. I'm not sure if they asked us whom we wanted to live with, but if I was asked I would have surely said Mom, without even needing to consider it. And my sister felt just the same, I'm sure, about Dad.

Whatever his motivation was, Dad took my sister away. And I missed her, her tough play alternating with princess neediness, her cruelty even. She had always been angry, since she was a baby even, but she was mine, and I needed her. We were each other's witness. Now we would have to face our pain in private, and it felt wrong.

When I was alone I imagined her near me. When Mom gave me waffles as a treat now I'd paste over every square with butter like I'd seen her do in oblivious indulgence. I would go visit them on weekends sometimes and it seemed like she had it good. She always had new things, newer clothes, better movies and video games, and whatever food she wanted, all of which was restricted for me, for both moral and financial reasons. I envied her but I also didn't; it all seemed a little wrong somehow, her world. She had a new bunk bed whose beams were made to look like giant pastel pencils. She had a poster of a perfect red Corvette on her wall, and another one of Kirk Gibson, clutch home-run hitter for the Tigers. Dad's favorites.

Sometimes Dad would kick her back to us for months at a time as punishment, or maybe to loosen himself from her care during gambling binges. A preteen now, she abused me even more harshly, and I withdrew from her. We only came together to fight. There was the time a neighbor called the cops when he saw, from his kitchen window, her pressing a foot into my neck after having thrown me down on the sidewalk outside of our apartment complex. I'd gone limp and unresponsive, but when I woke up to the faces above me I said I was fine, nothing happened, I fell. There was constant hitting, bruises, insults. I was patient, and soft, always. I never fought back. For one thing, she had that maniacal strength particular to a preteen girl with nothing to lose. And the other thing was that I knew, even as a child, that even if he never touched her, Dad was hurting her worse than she could hurt me.

I didn't know what I was seeing when I looked at my dad and my sister together. I don't think children can always recognize abuse, especially private, isolated instances in a context of otherwise normal family behavior. But I remember knowing one thing was wrong: the way he talked to her. After losing a softball game (he coached her team) he didn't say the things I knew a parent should say after a loss about doing your best, being a good sport, thinking about how to improve next time. I sat in the backseat of the car while he took us home from one loss, in pained silence. She was crying. He berated her, disparaged her teammates, mocked her for being a girl, for being a child. This time, seeing it right, I finally spoke up. "It wasn't *her* fault they lost."

"What do *you* know about it? Huh? Keep out of this," he snapped. I retreated. And I left her there, in his line of fire, while I slipped away into my own world, which was quieter and safer than hers. It's guilt now, of course it's guilt, and I can't help but wonder if there was more I could have done for her.

She grew and settled into a singular focus of pleasing him; a difficult and heartbreaking pursuit for a little girl. They seemed more like a strange, uneven couple than a father and daughter. At best, he just didn't know how to be a parent. He tried to impress her, lying about knowing everything, or showing off in childish ways. She followed. He outfitted her in boy clothes and a short spiny-top mullet. In photos you'd think she was my brother.

"Butch and Spike," Dad would call us all the time, "that's what I would've named you if you were boys." I'd groan with comic disgust but my sister played along. She'd laugh but then look distant, and I imagined her mentally straining to transform herself into Spike.

Then, in just a few years she filled in as a girl and had to embrace it, so she embraced it hard: as a preteen princess with waist-length hair and fake nails that made her look like a tough thirty-year-old. He dressed her up and brought her to the same Hazel Park racetrack he'd taken our mom on their first date. He taught her his tastes: have fun, look good, and spend money as loudly as possible.

"Your mother is a nutcase," he'd tell us while driving. "She belongs in the loony bin!" he'd say, lolling his tongue and turning his finger in a circle near his temple for emphasis. "What is she even feeding you there, granola and berries? She drops you off in the woods to pick your own berries for dinner?" He'd laugh lightly, then his mood would get dark and quiet. "She's sick. She's a sick person."

My sister went along with it, smiling and agreeing, sometimes joining in. I just stayed quiet and smiled dumbly, nodding sometimes instead of disagreeing just so the session would end sooner and we could talk about something else, or nothing. There is a particular feeling a child has when hearing one parent degrade the other parent. It's a kind of crushing, a cold spring of mistrust pierced open, even if it's all lies, and even if you think you don't care. I still wonder what happened to my sister when she lived with Dad. She says she doesn't remember much but she does have nightmares.

I told my sister, and no one else, that I was going to write about all of this eventually. We knew well what it felt like to be surprised by withheld facts, to be betrayed by our closest loved ones, so I was certain I shouldn't keep this from her. I was in Michigan for Thanksgiving, at Grandma's house, and finally found a moment alone with her when she volunteered to take the trash out after dinner. "I'll help!" I said, and popped up to follow.

We stood in the dark garage for a moment after finishing with the trash, watching a downpour soak the untended lawn in back. "I'm writing about things," I said.

She looked at me and tilted her head sympathetically. She knew what I meant. Her eyes went far away.

"I'm going to have a lot of questions for you," I said.

"Yeah. Well. OK. Like what?" She was wary, but willing to go where I was going.

"Well, you remember when they divorced the second time, and we were split up? Do you remember that process? Like, did they ask you if you wanted to go with Dad, or did he just tell you it was happening?"

"I wanted to go with him. I think. I'm not sure if I was asked. But I remember Dad being really insistent that I live with him and not you guys, since Mom was crazy, and Dad didn't much like you."

I laughed a little. "I didn't much like him either." We looked back at the rain through the garage door window. I continued, "Who knows. Mom said he wanted you to go with him so he wouldn't have to pay child support."

She fell a little in her posture and looked down. I should not have said that, I realized. Even if it was true, even if it was something she apparently didn't know, she didn't *need* to know this new hurtful thing, I realized. She said she wasn't surprised and tried to seem fine about it, but I could see the disappointment. It was something I saw in her a lot, the way she'd press her lips together firmly like shutting something out, or in. *Maybe it is not better to say everything*, I thought.

26

In photographs of them as children, my sister and my mom are indistinguishable. My sister has Mom's flawless, almost-olive skin, her dark, shiny thick hair, dainty nose, perfect smile, rich brown eyes, pure symmetry, and feminine balance. My sister once won Miss Photogenic in a teen beauty pageant, which I attended against my will, my own face buried in a library book I had brought for the duration of the spectacle.

I look nothing like my sister. I have Dad's moony Polish face, pale ruffles of hair, eyes too big and round, like a poor doll, verge-of-tears dark bluegreen and sad. Even at rest, my eyes convey a naturally solemn and far-off expression that perpetually draws "What's wrong?" from boyfriends and strangers, even when I am happy. You would never think we were sisters.

27

A pile of dusty eye shadow shells and tubes of Wet n Wild lipsticks with their pink innards concussed against their clear caps mounded between us as my sister and I sat on the floor, dipping spongy applicators into pods of color or drawing streaks of lipstick on the backs of our fists.

I raised a vivid blue eyeliner pencil to her eyes, warily, holding my breath. Feathering little strokes next to her lashline, boiling inside over her perfect almond-shaped eyes and perfect nose.

"See, your eye." I held up a mirror. "*This* is the color you want? It looked better before." She examined.

"No, retard. This is how it is *supposed* to look," she said, one dark perfect eye rimmed now with the insane blue, how her eyes were supposed to look.

"Look at your nose. It's perfect." I squashed it with my thumb and she shook her head away, peering back into the mirror.

"It's just normal, I don't know."

"Look at mine." She looked.

"Oh." She didn't try to not wince. She had never looked before, I could see.

A fifty-dollar bill drifted between us like a leaf and landed over our pile of cheap makeup. "Ta-dah!"

Dad was standing over us, a cigarette-pack-sized wad of folded bills in his hand. We looked at the fifty, then back up at him, blankly, not sure what this meant. "Split it, girls. Go get more makeup or something. Have a makeup party or something. Right?" He made a Donald Duck laugh.

My sister grabbed the bill and widened her eyes, exhibiting the excitement Dad was looking for, bouncing a little and now waving the bill like a flag. Dad laughed again and shuffled off to his bedroom and closed the door. She stood up and scootched her feet into her flip-flops. "Enough time to walk to the drugstore before stupid Mom gets here to pick you up. Lezz go!" she said, like Dad.

I slumped closer to the makeup pile, idly tossing aside crazed blush pods and tubes of concealer with the writing worn away. "What do you even need?"

She stomped over and grabbed my ponytail, yanking it up until I stood. "COME. ON. Brat. Maybe you can find something to fix your ugly face."

28

The face of a gorilla blacked out the window in the kitchen door. I squealed and my friends squealed in response.

I undid the dead bolt and threw the door open and the gorilla took his cue. "Haaaaaaaaaappy birthdaytoyou! Happy happy happy! Birthday birthday birthdaaaaayyyyy! To YOUUUUUUU!" The gorilla sang with a fake operatic frog voice and extended a single rose to me with a tiny card attached. It said:

> No monkeying around—it's your birthday! Happy
> 13th Molly!
> > Love,
> > Dad

We cracked up—embarrassed, delighted. Applauded when the song was over. The man in the gorilla suit shifted his weight around neurotically, hyped up, looking at us girls. He tugged at his giant red bowtie and shook the gorilla head mask loosely. His real voice was scratchy and high. "Hey what you girls doing tonight, huh? Having a party? Party time?" We laughed in that pitying way girls do when they don't like you. The man in the gorilla suit from the singing telegram service Dad had hired pried at his eyeholes to wipe the sweat around his eyes with his nasty furry finger. This was the kind of birthday gift Dad would give me—distant, hands-off—but I was delighted to get anything at all. The gorilla suit was close to me now and it smelled like closets and cigarettes. "You girls wanna party?"

"Ummm, haha. My mom's coming to pick us up soon. Thanks for the song." I opened the door.

"OK, ladies, OK. Hey, happy birthday, baby girl. Yeah, girl. Can I get a hug? Birthday huuuuggg??" The gorilla opened his gross arms. My friends tittered nervously.

I hugged the gorilla, laughing.

29

Three months later, Dad was arrested. My sister was fifteen that summer. She was there when it happened—I wasn't. It was something I was told about. Told by Mom, told by cops, told by reporters just like everyone else watching the news was told.

A story. A story like a dark new house we had to move to.

Mom and I now lived in a condo her parents had helped her buy in a humble complex on Ironwood Street in Rochester, where we'd stay for four years—my longest tenure anywhere. I'd go all the way through high school without having to move, because, I realized later, Dad, the disrupting factor in our lives, would be in prison after this summer.

It was nearing the end of the summer and my mom and I had just come home from a vacation—although at the time, as a preteen, camping was not "vacation" but pointless traveling drudgery. We were tired from the drive back from Canada and dirty from the weeklong camping and hiking trip along the coast of Georgian Bay in Lake Huron, swimming briefly in the icy water or taking glass-bottomed boat tours of old shipwrecks. Mom pressed the blinking button on the answering machine and I dragged my bag upstairs to unpack. In my small room I dumped my stinky clothes out and just sat for a moment, listening to the muffled sound of Mom on the phone downstairs. Then I started listening to it. Her voice was getting louder and sharper. I had already moved back toward the stairs when she called my name.

She sat at the kitchen table, the extra-long curly phone cord stretched to her as she held the receiver with her thumb on its button. Her voice was keyed high with exasperation. "That was Grandpa. Your father has been arrested and your sister is staying with them."

I paused for a while, staring calmly. "What did he do?"

"Robbed banks." She looked at me and we didn't say anything. She hadn't tensed up or pinched her face in anger. In fact, her face cleared out flat, like the look of someone who's just remembered something.

"Robbed banks?" I finally said.

"Robbed banks," she repeated dreamily. "Bank robbery. Huh. You don't say," she murmured to herself, nodding blankly.

It didn't feel like some kind of mistake, like it sometimes feels when you don't want to believe what's happened. It was horrible how easy it was to accept. Almost funny. In the pressurized silence the beginnings of a laugh could have crept over me, but I fought it.

The room felt as dark and solid as iron. I didn't cry or scream. I remember standing still for a while in the kitchen, looking at the linoleum floor and saying nothing, feeling like I was waiting for instructions. In some ways I felt this was good. I probably felt some relief. He'd be removed from our lives in an official and secure way. It solved him in a way none of us could. He was exposed, finally, made into something specific: a bank robber. It was terrifying, for sure, but satisfying in how *pinned down* Dad suddenly was in this moment.

I wasn't scared or shocked. I think partly because I was a thirteen-year-old girl and I already hated the world and felt like it hated me, so there was nothing it could do to surprise me. Dad especially could not surprise me. Any story could've fit him. In fact, Mom and I were waiting for his story, and here one was. In the moment, I would say we were both very pleased with it.

We didn't say much. We both knew it was a big moment. Everything would soon be different for us, but for now we just sat with the last of our old reality. I stared out of the window in the kitchen, into the normal day outside. Eventually Mom went upstairs to take a shower and shut herself in her bedroom.

Helpless, I plopped in front of the TV and turned it on. The first of the evening news was just coming on, something

I would normally turn away from, but I froze when I saw his face. My dad's mug shot floating in the corner next to the familiar Local 4 reporter, a reporter who was talking about him, saying his last name, my last name, a breaking story, but I couldn't hear, the sound disappeared. I could only see his face, sad face, baggy eyes, deep frown, Dad.

30

My sister had been dropped off by her friend that evening, around dinnertime, after Dad failed to respond to her pages. There were cop cars in the parking lot of their condo complex. The door was wide open. She walked straight in and said hello.

People in black jackets and black FBI hats swarmed her, wanted to know who she was, what she knew, if she knew of any money anywhere, any guns. She was alone, fifteen years old. They were the ones to tell her what happened. They kept her in the dining room, away from the rest of the condo, which they were ripping apart.

They showed her photos of him from the bank security cameras. At first she didn't recognize him. The photos were grainy and he had on sunglasses and a moustache. "Is this your dad?"

She looked, carefully. They flipped through more photos. At the sight of one, she sighed.

"That's my hat. My U of M hat. I was wondering where that was." She slumped in the chair, crying, now certain. A dad wearing his daughter's hat during a bank robbery: a photo of this happening. My sister felt some relief too in that moment, seeing the photo, knowing something about him for certain.

The agent told her to call someone and pack a bag.

Mom and I weren't there. She didn't know we'd gone camping. She kept calling and hanging up, the clicks recorded on our answering machine for us to find later.

Eventually she called Grandpa, and he came to get her. As soon as they got back to Grandpa's house, Dad called.

I asked her about this call recently. What did he possibly have to say for himself in that phone call?

"He wanted to know what happened. Not to me, but to his stuff. He kept asking if they went through his stuff, if they looked in his room. I said yes, obviously, Dad. He was annoyed with that only, said they had no right to do that or that it was illegal or something. I asked him if he did this, what they said he did, the robberies. He said no. Mistaken identity. I said, 'I saw the photo of you, Dad, wearing *my* hat while robbing a bank.' Not me, he said. He was totally calm on the phone. He dismissed it all in a funny way, like it was all a big joke," she told me.

Mom drove us to Grandma and Grandpa's house while I asked questions. She said she knew he'd lost his job at GM a few months earlier and she'd been wondering where he'd been getting his money. He'd lost his job over a car. Dad gave my sister a red Corvette in the spring as an early fifteenth-birthday present. She'd been driving it to school on her learner's permit and was pulled over on a trip home. They didn't tell her why, just put her in the back of the cop car and took her to the station. They called Mom to explain: the car was stolen, come pick up your daughter.

It was a company car; Dad took it off the lot at the Tech Center without permission. It was reported stolen and Dad was fired. He'd been attempting to appear busy for two months.

My sister said she noticed he was around a lot. He'd pick her up from school unexpectedly. Take her out to eat almost every night. He bought a cell phone for himself. He bought a new watch for himself. No job, but looser with money than ever before. And now that the ill-gotten Corvette was gone, he bought her a car: a used blue Pontiac Firebird. He'd just dropped it off to have the windows tinted.

That night we sat with my grandparents and just talked, asked each other questions until there was nothing else to say. In the dark living room it would go quiet for a while, and Grandpa would ask, "But why would he do this?" and Mom would say, "Because he needed money!" and the room would go quiet again. Then Grandpa would ask the question again.

My sister sat quietly. She didn't look stunned. She looked angry. She chewed her fingernails and said nothing, just boiled, apart from us.

We found out more when the story was reported on the late news. They said he had robbed banks all summer, eleven in all, and the FBI had been tracking him for a while, staking out banks, hoping to catch him at one.

First he'd rent a car. Then drive to a hotel. He'd take the license plate off the rental, and switch it with any nicer-looking car in the hotel lot. He'd drive to a bank, wait a bit in the car, watching the bank, looking for a calm moment.

After the robbery he'd switch the license plates back, then go out for a meal or round of golf.

I saw grainy gray photos of him from the security cameras of a bank. He had on a hat and glasses and a large fake moustache, but I could see his mouth and chin and I knew it was him. He looked like he does when he is certain of himself. An iron calm. He had no gun. Tellers reported that he pointed something at them from inside the pocket of his jacket, probably his finger or a toy gun. He'd wait in line, and calmly slide a withdrawal slip under the window onto which he'd written *ACT NORMAL. This is a robbery, give me all the bills in your drawer.* The tellers passed him money, and he left, acting normal, just as he wanted it to be. The customers around him went about their business, oblivious. It just looked like a withdrawal to the other customers in line.

When he was caught after the last robbery, one newspaper article reported that he said he was relieved to be caught. Would he really have said that? I doubted a lot of the facts in the flurry of articles about him; many were wrong. In his pockets were chips from Windsor Casino and betting slips from the Hazel Park Raceway, where he'd brought my mom on their very first date, and where he later brought my sister on weekend nights as a treat.

My sister faithfully clipped every newspaper article she could find about him and kept them in a scrapbook. At the time I honestly couldn't tell if she was proud or disgusted. I asked her recently if she still had the clippings, but she said no, said she threw away everything of his.

I had kept one clipping, only because I thought it was funny that there were so many errors about us in it—that we were eight and nine, and it had our names wrong. I had stuck it into my scrapbook, among goofy snapshots of me and my friends in middle school. It was just there, out of place.

31

" It's 'game over' for the Super Mario Brothers Bandit, the Rochester man charged with allegedly robbing ten banks in Macomb and Oakland Counties since June 22 . . ."

Dad's face hung on the TV screen over the shoulder of the newscaster. For weeks after his arrest the media followed the story, updating us on his charges—both state and federal. I wonder if they would have followed up at all if it hadn't been for his goofy nickname.

Someone on his case at the FBI thought he looked like Mario, with the bushy fake moustache and suspenders under his jacket and the flat newsboy cap he'd sometimes wear to the robberies. Mario, from *my* game. Super Mario Bros. 3 was my favorite game at the very time he was arrested; I played it almost every day on my Nintendo after school.

I switched from the news to my Nintendo. I played it even more after his arrest. It was the best one of the Mario Bros., the one with the raccoon tail, the frog suit, the vivid blue skies, and faces on all the clouds and trees—the cheeriest installment of the series. Unlikely that I was looking for him; more likely that I simply wanted to withdraw even further from my few friends. Still, there he was, in the game, every time I turned it on.

There was the seriousness of what he did against the silliness of this detail, and how this nickname came to represent him in the media and among strangers as a clownish criminal. I wanted to join in this rousing dismissal of him too. I didn't join in anywhere, though, not all the way. My sister remained on his side, hoping, somehow, that it would all turn out to be some kind of mistake like he said it was. Mom never was on his side, and seemed to feel comfortable with his dismissal. I just kept quiet.

Often I leave that detail about his nickname out of the story now when I tell people. Tonally, the story becomes confusing if I mention his nickname. I start to smile and laugh sometimes, and the listener feels confused in what emotion to present. I might have to explain how it was not just any video-game character they assigned to my father, but my favorite one, the *main one* in my world—what a coincidence. How could my dad's arrest be both awful and hilarious at the same time? Two opposing sharp points, irreconcilable. It hurt. But it was absurd, so I could laugh.

32

The face of Mr. Blue, West Middle School's choir teacher, was turning purple with rage, as usual. The altos were talking and it was now the eighth time we'd gone over this section of Chicago's "You're the Inspiration." He wanted us to sing the notes straight, without bending them like the singer does in the recorded version we all knew. In the soprano section I was watching the clock; soon I'd be saved from this.

"Molly?" It was Mrs. B, school counselor, come to retrieve me for my weekly session. In 1993 my seventh-grade year was launched with a hush around school I could feel—people talking, but not talking to me. The only person who approached me directly—had to, I suppose—was the counselor. I was relieved to get out of choir and walk with her through the quiet halls to her office.

"Jeez. You have so much stuff in your pockets!" She looked at the huge pockets on the baggy men's corduroy pants I was wearing, straight from Value Village, packed with stuff. "What's in there," she said more seriously.

"Oh, just . . . lipstick, pens, compact, gum, sunglasses . . ." How strange to hold the attention of an adult! But now, only out of suspicion. I was embarrassed.

In her office I was supposed to be a wreck, have a breakdown, or at least cry. "What Cold Pricklies have been visiting you this week?" she asked, handing me a navy blue plastic shape with points protruding from it and googly eyes glued to its center. This was the Cold Prickly. In her lap, the Warm Fuzzy, a pink furry ball with similar eyes glued to it, waited.

"I didn't . . . meet any . . . Cold Pricklies this week," I responded quietly. She looked blankly at me, holding a smile, as if I had not said anything yet. I looked at the photos of her kids hung on the walls, the bowl of autumnal potpourri below, the small teddy bears. She'd always wait as long as it took until I said what she wanted to hear, I knew. Eventually I'd just offer the narrative she was looking for so I could end these sessions. But this time, I held out.

"I can't give you a Warm Fuzzy if you don't let go of a Cold Prickly first!" she explained cheerily. I looked at the clock. Maybe this wasn't better than the purple face of Mr. Blue.

"OK, um. Let's see. I feel lonely."

"Lonely! You aren't lonely. You have friends! Your friend Lindsey. And your mom and your sister, and me, I'm your friend! Now, see, doesn't the thought of all your friends around

119

you give you a Warm Fuzzy?" She moved the pink creature from her lap and placed it in mine while I perfunctorily offered the Cold Prickly back.

"Do you know what *alienated* means?" I looked at the clock. "It means you feel separated from your world. And your dad, well, I imagine how upsetting it must be to learn he committed such an out-of-character crime. You are feeling alienated from him right now, your own father, the person you trusted the most—snapped!"

And that was the story. She, along with everyone else, swallowed it whole. He was presented in the news, in court, and in conversation as a meek, diligent autoworker with no record who *must have* just suddenly snapped. They turned over reasons why such a normal man might choose to commit such an out-of-character crime: gambling addiction, his hours at the plant being cut, post-traumatic stress disorder from the Vietnam War, Detroit itself. At first I wondered if they knew something I didn't.

"No," I said.

"No?"

"No. That isn't how I feel. And that's not my dad's story. *And* I know enough about therapy to know that you're not supposed to tell me how I feel or don't feel. My mom is a therapist, you know. I've been in therapy since I was six. I know the deal."

Mrs. B squinted at me and smiled. I tossed the Warm Fuzzy from one hand to the other, waiting.

"You're a smart cookie, Molly. But you don't know the deal."

The bell rang and a flood of students shuffled through the halls. I returned Mrs. B's Warm Fuzzy to her and thanked her, joining the moving crowd.

I didn't know the deal. I didn't know anything. But I knew that the official story everyone else had bought about my dad wasn't right. I thought about it through algebra, through chemistry. How does one do anything "out of character"? Character, I reasoned, *is* action. It is *exactly* defined by the actions one takes—especially in crisis. Dad had been fired. He was out of money. Bookies were calling in his debts—I tried to imagine the pressure, the fear. He could have asked for help. Right? That's what you're supposed to do when you're in trouble—go to your brothers and sisters, your partners, your friends. I tried to imagine Dad humbling himself before anyone in his life and I couldn't. *This* is *his character*, I thought. *There it is, plain as day.*

At lunch I headed for the library, set in the center of the school. I walked through the stacks, looking for something new. If character is action, what does it say about *us* that we needed to construct this digestible story about him—mild man, suddenly snapped? My fingers ran along the spines of young adult fiction. The story means we are storytellers, that's all.

The story makes things easier for us: solves a mystery, the problem of *why*. And maybe to call an act "out of character" is to reveal *oneself*: how limited any one person's knowledge is of any other person. Some people's wall of privacy is quite opaque, but that doesn't mean what's behind it is not part of them. No, the "out-of-character" story is just a barren and cartoonish way of thinking about character.

I moved across the aisle to the poetry section and set my fingers on the oldest-looking book on the shelf. *Leaves of Grass*. I pulled it down and opened to the center of the book:

> *And go lull yourself with what you can understand,*
> *   and with piano-tunes,*
> *For I lull nobody, and you will never understand me.*

I snapped the book shut as if I'd seen something in it move. My life turned on a pivot point when I read these lines from the end of "To a Certain Civilian." It seemed like *poetry itself* speaking to me in those lines, challenging me to come to new ground. I didn't turn back to the fiction section that year. Poetry became my companion, starting with Whitman, then Dickinson, then the rest of that small section. It seemed to know a better way to the world—an approach more honest, more direct, sharper.

I enfolded a deep mistrust of stories into my being that year. It was personal. It was, in a way I didn't know yet, political. I mean I saw this story on the news, this *same* story about my dad that my family and friends were telling themselves.

I watched the story spill forth. From the inner state of my particular sister and mom and grandparents came a certain story about Dad to soothe themselves with, then the story made its way outward, to the cops, the FBI, the reporters. I saw how a public narrative starts with *one person*—my sister, for example, thinking, talking, grasping for old stories to lay atop new ones; then reinforcement occurs, corners are cut, subtlety lost, and the story becomes history: a story that doesn't cultivate contemplation but preempts it, ends it, like a coarse mask.

I laughed about it with my friends—Lindsey and Lauren, and my best friend Noah. They watched me carefully and wanted to know how they could help, but I offered nothing, and they gave up their concern eventually. I started to know then what I know now: *why* is a hard question. Sometimes it's the wrong question to try to work out.

Still, I've tried working on *why* ever since. I dug up old court records from his first trial, looking for transcripts, for things he said on record that could explain his actions. I wasn't surprised when I came across his lawyer's sentencing memo from the trial, in which he used this exact reasoning in asking for lighter sentencing from the judge: "This is one of those rare cases where an individual who would otherwise be the last person you would suspect of threatening harm to others, did something completely out of character for reasons that are hard to fathom."

The reasons weren't that hard to fathom. He wanted to keep going. What everyone wants. I felt certain I didn't know him, but I knew there was a lot I couldn't see. Or, I should say, I knew there was a darkness. I was around his darkness.

123

I was as close to it as a child could be to her father's darkness without seeing it.

I carried on with West Middle School, keeping quiet, reading poetry. Others had it worse, I knew, much worse. Therapists have told me it is not productive to compare trauma and rate its value as "worse" or "better" than other trauma, but I am just being practical. I was not raped or starved or maimed, just ignored, and I lived OK in that empty space. I can come up with lots of reasons to make it OK.

My mom and I took my sister back to their condo to get more of her belongings. Over the next few weeks we'd go back there to take things to keep or sell. When we first arrived the FBI had just sacked the place again looking for the money or evidence. The money was all gone, though, paid to his debtors, spent on overdue bills, or wasted. Eleven banks, and all together he'd stolen only about $44,000.

It seemed like the FBI had cut open everything possible: the couches, pillows, mattresses, suitcases, boxes of food, bags of whatever, all of her stuffed animals. Photo albums were flung open in a pile on the kitchen table. All of my sister's clothes were thrown from her closet and drawers into the center of her room. His room was worse. Nothing was OK. The white stuffing from his comforter had been pulled out like guts. It was awful for my sister, to see her home ripped open in every way, all for money. It seemed cruel, weirdly vengeful, although it probably wasn't. I felt guilty for not being her. I felt sick that I lived with Mom instead of Dad and this didn't happen to me. It did happen to me—but I was on the farther side of things. I hated that about myself.

She packed up her clothes and things of hers that weren't destroyed. She cried, the destroyed one, plucking framed photos of her and Dad together from the wall and hugging them like a war widow. Most of the rest of the stuff would be thrown out. The only things I took were a cheap record player and his Italian opera records. I also took what I thought were blank cassettes, but later I discovered they were full of recordings from the radio or CDs he liked. One had the Simply Red version of "If You Don't Know Me By Now" recorded over and over, back-to-back, the entire tape.

33

They let my sister keep the Firebird because, she argued to the FBI, he owed her money. They couldn't exactly trace the car to stolen money anyway. She kept the Firebird all through high school until she got into a fight with some girl over a boy, and the car's paint job ended up disfigured after being dotted with bologna in the school parking lot. She sold it for almost nothing.

She stayed with our grandparents for a few weeks, then came to stay with us. For the one year we went to the same high school—her as a senior and me as a freshman—she'd sometimes drive me to school in that car. At 7:15 a.m. I'd squash myself into the backseat and push my nose into my coat sleeve or cardigan or whatever I had to filter the overpowering stink of shitty perfume she'd just doused her entire upper body in moments before plopping into the driver's seat, barely awake, sometimes hungover. In the cold dark mornings I'd go with her like that, my whole chest vibrating from the dumb bass of 2 Live Crew chanting "pop that pussy" or "put your back into it" while I tried to cover myself from all of it, especially her, her like this. Mostly I walked to school.

My sister moved in with us on a Sunday and the FBI came to see her the next day. I remember letting them in. It was sunny and warm and the two men filled the door completely with darkness. Mom led them to the kitchen table, where my sister was waiting for the interview, this same kitchen where Dad had sent a singing gorilla just a few months before. Not needed, I sat secretly on the steps to listen. "Do you recognize the man in this photo?" one of them began.

"Yeah that's my Uncle Mike." My sister's voice was icy.

"Your Uncle Mike has been coming around a lot lately, hasn't he?"

"No."

"You saw him visiting your dad a lot last week, didn't you? Answer calls from him too?"

"Um no, not at all."

"Do you recognize the man in this photo?"

"No."

It was an army buddy Dad knew in Vietnam. They showed her a yellowy photo of them in fatigues, smoking, clasped to each other over a machine gun on a tripod as if the three of them were posing for a family portrait. Mom watched the interviewers and my sister with concern.

"And this man here, next to your dad, you recognize him, don't you?"

"I already told you, that is Uncle Mike," she said, angry now.

"And here?"

"I. Don't. Know." She was muffling tears. They kept asking her over and over to identify either Uncle Mike or the war buddy, or sometimes Dad in surveillance video stills. Mom was getting agitated too.

"OK, that's enough. She doesn't know anything, for Christ's sake, she wasn't *there*," Mom interrupted. "She's just a child."

Dad told the investigators he'd been framed, that it was either this old war buddy or his brother who'd done the robberies, not him. He blamed his own brother. There was the money in his car, the disguise, the security camera photos of him coming and going from the banks, his face clear as day. *Framed.* Nothing much came of this claim, ultimately, except a couple of hour-long FBI interviews my sister pressed herself through.

Our first trip back to Dad's condo Mom saw a fake ID he was making on his desk, the materials laid out plainly, almost comically obvious: an X-Acto knife, a new name, another photo. He must have been planning to take off. There is no return to a normal life after a crime spree, is there? I can't imagine he thought he could just quit robbing and go back to a real job, back to normal. I also don't know why he didn't split sooner. He could've brought my sister to us, to get her out of the way at least. He could've taken his money and moved away, to start over as a new man. But he just came home, kept coming home after the robberies, pretending everything was normal. Perhaps he was hesitating, or waiting to save up more money. Maybe he didn't want to leave my sister. Or he was lazy, or scared.

I didn't go to any of the trial or court appearances with my mom and sister. I never saw him at all during that time. The news covered the story, and I'd see photos of him in the paper or the court sketches on the local news. Dad's face looked sour, saggy. I threw myself harder into school and tried to forget the mess. I wanted to become a chemist. I loved the formulas and codes. It seemed grand and safe, things to know, plain and tidy and logical.

I could forget. I forgot.

There seemed to be nothing to gain from thinking about it. I couldn't help him, or my sister, or myself, by thinking about it, so I turned away.

The local media continued to cover the drawn-out trials, dragged out by Dad's insistence on a psychological evaluation, then rounds of firing his lawyers. It would pop up sometimes on the news or in newspapers. My sister followed them more closely.

He wanted to plead insanity, claim that the trauma from PTSD caused his actions, which he described as out-of-body experiences, with no memory of them. His first lawyer was fired for strongly urging him not to take this course of action. After all, he had kept a neat list of the robberies, which was in his wallet when he was arrested, noting the time, date, and amount of money procured from each one. Not exactly consistent with an "out-of-body experience."

After long delays, constant objections, and legal stalling, he was evaluated by a court psychiatrist, deemed competent, and had to drop his insanity defense. He was sentenced to ten years for felony bank robbery, but would serve only seven with good behavior.

He never gave in. Never admitted his crimes, never apologized. Not publicly nor privately, not to anyone. His story of being framed dropped away, as did the story of the amnesia and war trauma, until there was just silence, just him there with his crimes, with no stories to explain them, just silence.

34

When Dad was arrested I had been camping grumpily with Mom, but afterward, everything was different. Suddenly I liked camping. I wanted to go every chance I could. With Mom, with boyfriends, alone sometimes. It was Mom's coping mechanism, and I took it up too. As a teenager, I rode my bike across the top half of Michigan's Lower Peninsula, alone, sleeping in cheap campgrounds and stopping in small towns to eat. I just wanted the air to push clear through me across farmland and mines of old glacial plains, land that was still rising, bouncing back a few centimeters every year from the pressure of long-gone ice sheets six thousand feet high. Gentle moraines ended in dunes on Lake Michigan, which I reached in a week, then unceremoniously I turned to circle back.

Having stopped on a very empty stretch for a drink and a rest, I watched a pickup truck slow on the shoulder in front of me and stop. I felt a sick cringe in my gut. Not a person or house for miles. The door popped open and I climbed onto my bike. A man with dead eyes, in overalls and a trucker hat, moved toward me with some mumbled questions: "You OK out here . . . you need a lift? I'll putcher bike in the back . . ." I was already pushing off on my heavily loaded bike. I passed him wide but still he made a weird grab for my arm. With no weapon, I'd thought to at least pull my camera out and snap a photo of his license plate, just to scare him, I guess. He didn't follow me.

It was robustly unsafe alone out there, but I didn't think about it. I loved the Great Lakes and I wanted to be near them. Their spans were calmer and colder than the ocean, fresh-feeling, but dizzyingly wide against the horizon. Unlike anywhere else in the world. Lake Superior was my favorite: deep and clear down to the rocks, too cold to grow the regular lake muck I'd felt in the smaller interior lakes dotting Michigan, chilly a few steps out of the shallows, even in summer. Shipwrecks and petrified forests were preserved below. You could just look down and see them in the deep, still as tombs. Michigan was my body, surrounded by small, secret oceans that pulled on me, from the inside out.

On that bike trip I camped illegally on a small cove on Huron's shore, a plot in the middle of nowhere, circled by thick pines. There was nothing to do those nights, and I loved it. Before dark I'd lie on the dune grass and watch the pine tops sway in the darkening patch of sky. I would lie still for so long. I imagined my body collapsing, sinking in, the grass creeping over, these tall trees pinioning it, the rusty needle bed that'd blanket me, the leathery dead cottonwood leaves in drifts, then snow pack, the particular blue hush of it in northern pine stands, the mud of a bog encroaching, my body thinning its parts and trickling down, lake water washing its particles out, down among billion-year-old minerals, into the compressed coals of ancient plants, ancient places, down to the basalt, where it belongs, part of the dirt and sand, safe, in an honest home; how happy that made me to imagine.

35

The intensity of the event faded and Dad faded in my life. I let him fade. For my sister, his presence seemed to become even more intense, now disembodied, like a ghost following her everywhere, reaching her through letters and phone calls. He tried to parent her through his letters; I found some of them in the basement of my sister's house when I was looking for the scrapbooks full of newspaper clippings she'd kept. "It's all yours," she said, gesturing to the basement, when I had asked her if I could look at any "Dad stuff" she had kept. "But I don't want to talk about it." The scrapbooks were gone but manila folders full of his letters had been kept alongside bank statements in her filing cabinets.

In the letters it's clear that her behavior was wild now; she was a party girl, checked out at school, dating a trashy older guy who was into drag racing. Dad hated this guy and tried, in his letters, to forbid her from seeing him. Most of the letters admonished her for the trouble she was getting herself into, which she must have been confessing to in her letters to him, oddly. She was being honest with him about her life at a time when she didn't *have* to be. She moved in with her scuzzy boyfriend, for a while at least, until he started hitting her and stealing from her. It was that story anyone would expect—an insecure girl acting out at her daddy, exactly that. Dad threatened her with all he had left: their relationship. He told her he'd never speak to her again unless she did what he wanted.

It went on like this for years. Invisible, he loomed huge in her life; he was all around her, emotionally, psychologically.

Toward the end of his term, my sister started to straighten up. She was hyperaware of his impending release and prepared for it, I think, with honest hope and incredible forgiveness. He is instructive in his letters, involved, advising my sister to transfer from a community college to the local university, telling her to take out student loans he promises to pay back when he gets out, instructing her on how to cheat on her taxes. My sister must have asked him about some family history, because in a few of the letters he gives a very different account of our parents' marriage. I know not to believe his version. But after all this time it is sort of nice just to hear him address it at all, the irony of his attitude toward our mom, surely, unfathomably, lost on him. He wrote:

> I'm glad you had a heart-to-heart with your
> mother. The way I see it, as a wife your mother

betrayed me (by sleeping with other men) and, more recently, as a friend she rejected me. I discarded the letter she wrote me otherwise I would send it to you and you could see in black and white where she tells me that she will have nothing to do with me. My "friend" betrayed me by breaking off our relationship.

You see, during these past five year, the word TRUST has taken on a new meaning for me. I know exactly who I can trust and all the other people I know mean nothing to me. You, the most important person in the world to me, and my sister Helen are the only ones I can trust. Thus, I must say that because your mother is a cheap whore I will never love her again. And, because your mother is self-centered and interminably dishonorable, I can never again be her friend.

Since you brought out some of the family past, I feel I must provide some of the facts from my perspective. First of all, I did have a gambling problem. I couldn't stay away from sports betting. I won a lot of money and I lost a lot of money. However, you were all the most important considerations in my life. Your mother didn't see it that way—she, in effect, was looking for an excuse to get out of a marriage that she felt trapped in. Be aware it was SHE who cheated on ME.

So you'll be living with her again. Please respect your biological relationship and remember this: you can never expect the real truth from her. She is a weak, untrustworthy person. Your mother is unable to teach you what true love is all about.

All of that aside, you really made my day on Father's Day. I started to feel low about it, but you came through and made me feel great. Your large envelope arrived yesterday and I would like to thank you, from the bottom of my heart, for all the wonderful surprises. Your greeting card brought tears to my eyes—I know you chose the words that were printed on it and all of them are greatly appreciated. The blown up, personalized photo is a terrific memento that I'll cherish forever and the copy of your report card couldn't have brought better news.

I guess Molly forgot about me. I shouldn't be surprised because she didn't think of me on my birthday either. Unless I hear from her belatedly I'll have to regard Molly like I do your half-sister ... self-centered and not concerned about Dad.

Love,

Dad

36

I tried, but often forgot to send him birthday cards during that period. Now I am much better about it, although it's a strange thing to shop for a birthday card for a dad in jail. The general sentiments of the dad birthday cards just don't apply but I sort through them anyway—*you were always there for me, dad* (no), *you taught me so much, dad* (no), *enjoy your cake and beer today, dad* (no), *another year of happy memories, dad* (no). I usually give up on the dad cards and settle on one that just says *Happy Birthday* inside.

August 2015 and Dad turned seventy in prison. I realized a week or so before his birthday. It would be a stretch to say we are close now, but we correspond. I remembered to buy a card with a gentle but distanced greeting. Then, I forgot.

The unsent card caught my eye on the kitchen table where I'd left it as I rushed out the door and it was too late: today was his birthday, I'd forgotten and now it was too late.

At my office I logged into CorrLinks, the federal prison bureau's email system, and wrote him a friendly message, hoping he would have a nice day, gently teasing him about being the big seven zero.

That night I checked CorrLinks again just to make sure the email went through this clunky prehistoric email service, and he'd already written back:

Dear Molly,

God bless you for remembering me. Yes, I turned 70 and nothing special happened here. Honestly, I feel like this is the wrong age for me—I certainly do not feel this old. The real problem is that I also feel that not much has been accomplished by me during the many years and I do not have enough time remaining to make up for wasted years (doing prison time). Thank you for the timely, lighthearted birthday greetings. It made my day.

Take care.

Love,

Dad

I don't know what to do with Dad's sentiments now. I don't know if they are real. And if they are real, I'm afraid of the new universe this would put me in: one in which I have a good dad, and this dad has a good daughter, and that's all there is—goodness.

37

I went through a phase where I would punch my mom in the stomach. Below the stomach, just under her belly button. Not hard. Mostly it would just surprise her. Even done very lightly she'd always buckle a little and make an "oof" noise. Sometime she'd laugh, but mostly she'd be annoyed, sometimes very angry. Whenever I saw her I'd do this, which wasn't very often.

Through high school I lived alone. Mom lived alone too, but in the same place. She was a therapist with a private practice now, specializing in addiction counseling, and she had clients all day, then group sessions at night. She existed in the contradictory space between doctor and patient, surviving with her own mental disorders to bear, holding me above water while she just barely kept afloat. I woke up before her to walk myself to school, then almost always went to bed before she came home. I ate cereal and canned soup or frozen vegetables with microwaved hot dogs. I brought in the mail, cleaned the condo, did laundry, played Nintendo, kept things going. I'd finish my homework diligently and go to sleep looking forward to school the next day. I loved school—the structure, the calm. I liked the bells and the facts and the tiny locker and the libraries, where I'd spend any time I had free. At home, food appeared in the fridge on weekends while I was out with my friends or hiking on the Paint Creek Trail.

Sometimes I wouldn't see her for a week or more. When I did see her it was in passing; she was always busy, in the middle of going somewhere, or dealing with some emotional story inside of her I didn't have access to. She had boyfriends who came and went, medication to start or stop. At the time I think I meant the stomach punching in a joking way. I feel sick thinking about this now. I don't think I knew I was angry about anything until recently.

"Manic bipolar," she told me one day when I asked her why the pansies had all been torn out of the pots in back. She explained the illness to me with clinical detachment. I thought about the unplanned camping trips she used to whisk me out of bed for on school days, the half-painted wall in one of my childhood bedrooms, never finished, the inexplicable shaking and crying, the days she spent locked in her bedroom. My life with her as a teenager was precarious—I never knew when she'd tilt and send our quiet, orderly life off the rails.

I saw my mom in hospital beds so many times, pulled back from a death she thought she wanted over and over—I can't say how many times she attempted suicide while I was in high school. She used to joke about it, say at night she hoped maybe this time she'd "wake up dead," and I would laugh with her, a little.

I remember the feeling in the hospital room when we'd visit her after another overdose attempt, her in the bed, zoned out and slow. I sat with her once, alone somehow, while she dozed, an old woman in a wheelchair in the next room saying, "Help me. Help me. Help me. Help me."

She felt awful about it, and about me and my sister seeing her, but she'd smile. Charcoal pumped into her stomach after an overdose attempt would catch in her teeth; I'd see it when she smiled and talked. Many times I saw this. Or the amnesia and total weakness after multiple sessions of electroshock. It was supposed to jolt old patterns out of her brain, but it jolted everything out. Over the weeks all of it came creeping back.

In a way her bipolar disorder made me distrustful of her emotions. I learned that her bursts of positive energy were short-lived, like sugar highs followed by a crash, however much she'd insist it was a new phase or better path. Like when she decided she was going to sell candles to make extra money and spent hundreds of dollars on boxes full of them that sat in boxes in a closet. She just didn't have the social life or network of friends required for that kind of endeavor, and hadn't thought that through. I grew suspicious of her good moods, and sad at my own suspicions. I wanted her to be happy and I wanted her happiness to stick. But it didn't.

Feelings moved across her dramatically like sharp weather. Happiness was keyed always a little too high, the colors too bright, almost painful or frightening, her cheery energy. Despair was so severe it transformed her physically— she'd wander through our small place, tired, in a rumpled nightgown, as if moving through mud. I left the house a lot, hung out with friends in a park nearby, or stayed with them when I could. I kept quiet about it.

Weeks of relative calm were interrupted by strange visitors—clients of hers who were temporarily homeless. She'd invited them to stay in our basement, violating all guidelines of professional practice.

Once after school I heard crying in the basement. A note on the counter explained that Janet would be staying with us for a few days, just until she gets back on her feet. Janet was a bony alcoholic woman whose sole possession seemed to be an enormous carton of tampons she'd hug as she traipsed up and down the stairs. I had no interactions with Janet except for when she'd set off the fire alarm by smoking menthols in the basement and I'd have to come down to tell her to stop. She would respond by smearing the cigarette out on the bottom of her tennis shoe and gently crying.

Just a week or so after Janet disappeared I came home to find a faded yellow seventies-era Impala parked in Mom's spot. I stopped. Beethoven was blasting from our condo, rattling the windows. I entered and saw a note on the counter; "Jonas" was all it said. I moved to the living room to see a loopy Norwegian with a lazy eye lying on his back, howling along with the tune, a vodka bottle raised in each hand above him.

"Hi," I said in a loud and disappointed way.

He saw me and raised up to turn the volume knob down on the tuner, still holding a bottle in each hand. "Hi, leettle geirl! I'm Yonas, your mom freend." I smiled at him, terrified.

"I have to stay here a leetle while. My house, burned down, my house. I burned it down accident." Jonas swayed back and forth on the floor, not quite looking at me while he talked. He had stringy blond hair and smelled filthy. I politely excused myself and turned to leave, off to the park or to a friend's house, anywhere. Jonas lasted a month or so at our place until he took Mom's stereo to a pawnshop so he could buy booze. After that, visitors rarely stayed overnight.

Even in the worst lows, when she would mess up her meds or mix liquor with them and be out of it or end up in the hospital, I wasn't ashamed of my mom. She was brave and strong and wild, and lived beyond me, which I accepted. And no matter what, she always went to work. She was good at her job. She helped people.

I liked to ask her about her clients, because they always seemed so much worse off than us. I remember the story of the kleptomaniac who'd steal paperback books from the Meijer store and dump them in a trash can as soon as he was outside. The anorexic who'd serve herself only the small gelled egg of chicken broth that came in the package of Mrs. Grass powdered soup, my sister's favorite. She ate it whole, un-cooked, like a gummy salt gem.

One woman I still think about to this day. She was an only child of two parents who were also only children, and both were dead. The woman, then, had no family at all. No sisters, brothers, parents, aunts, uncles, cousins, grandparents, nephews, nothing. She was working as a secretary, no friends, having an affair with her boss, seeing my mom for depression. Not a single family member. Mom said she felt sorry for her, and as bad as things ever got with family life, she was glad to have one at least. I always liked that she said this, but I think I secretly felt differently. I imagined myself as this woman, completely untethered by blood to other humans, without obligation to bonds of family customs, or the roles of sister, cousin, aunt, niece, daughter. How different her holidays must have been, how tidy, and how single-minded her aspirations could be. No one would say they want that. Still, I'd catch myself daydreaming about her life, how peaceful it must have been.

38

Mom told me her first memory also happened on a stairwell. The cold, dusty back steps, alone, where she'd gotten lost and sat down in her lostness. She thinks she was only three years old. "Eventually I realized I would have to just get up and find my way out or I'd be sitting there crying forever.

"No one can find you in the dark anyway. You just have to walk yourself out," she added.

39

Mom left home at fifteen, for good, just walked away one February morning. Her dad dropped her off at a corner near her school and she just turned the other direction and kept going. She was wearing a skirt, knee socks, tennis shoes, sweater, coat, and had nothing on her but schoolbooks and some change. Walking slowly in the cold, aimless at first, she decided she'd walk all the way to the family cabin, three hundred miles north. Once she made it to Olivet, the next town north of Marshall, she knew for sure she wouldn't turn back. She hitchhiked some, telling her rides she was supposed to be meeting her family at the cabin, but that she had gotten lost. She made it to the cabin in the middle of the night, with no one around the lake for miles, no lights anywhere, just silent snow. For three days she survived in the unheated cabin by building an igloo of blankets in the living room and rationing out the half-box of saltines left in the pantry.

Her mind went foggy in weakness and hunger. She wrapped herself in blankets, tied them with fishing rope, and did nothing but look out onto the frozen lake. She made up a weird song to sing to herself, a song she has always remembered, and I have heard her sing, only to herself:

In the waters of Babylon, no fish swim in the sea
Above the waters of Babylon no birds fly in the sky
By the waters of Babylon I sit alone and cry
Beneath the waters of Babylon my soul goes to die.

How thick and bright I loved my mom when she told me this story. I almost buckled to the floor. It made me feel exposed in the connection. My loneliness bubbled up to meet hers, as if looking for kin.

The house where my mom grew up in Marshall, Michigan, was an old six-bedroom house, now run as a bed and breakfast, built on property owned by James Fenimore Cooper. She had three brothers, but kept to herself mostly, wandering the three-acre property, climbing pine trees until they bent, just swaying atop them, or talking to the cattle on the next property over. She read a lot and dreamed of being an artist. She loved being alone, like I did, and would shut herself into a dark cabinet for hours just to hum and think.

And lifelong sadness sprung from the roots in this house. She finally told her best friend that her eldest brother had been molesting her at night, in her bed, for years. The friend told her boyfriend, only fourteen years old all of them, but he called her and talked to her about it. He said, "Here's what you say to him. You say, 'You have to stop doing this. I will tell my parents if you don't.'" She said she'd needed someone to give her the words. And she told him to stop, and he did. I don't like seeing this uncle at family occasions. Quiet and unfriendly, he is unlike anyone else in the clan. I perceive his silence as strained or simmering, but I'm sure that is just my perception.

It's unclear how much her parents knew about the abuse, or believed it if they did know. Mom could take only a year of silence and denial in that imposing house before she chose to flee.

Probably she would've come back on her own, maybe called her parents soon to come get her. But they'd already sent a state trooper to check the cabin to see if she was there. When she opened the door to let him in, she said he grabbed her arm, and she didn't like it, so she snapped and threatened him with the hunting knife she had pulled from behind her back.

And she never went back to Marshall. She was a delinquent now, a runaway, brandishing a knife at a cop. Her parents struck a deal with the courts and got her into a hospital instead of juvenile detention. A good hospital, in fact, the Neuropsychiatric Institute at the University of Michigan Hospital. First she shuffled the halls of the adult women's ward in a Thorazine haze, waiting for a bed to open in the adolescent unit. "Thorazine kept you compliant," she told me. "It felt like your brain had been hit with a giant sledgehammer. Brainless, but walking around, like a zombie."

Diagnoses came and went with trends or with new doctors. First she was given the borderline personality disorder label that other troubled teens were getting in the mid sixties, then it changed to manic depressive/bipolar, which she kept for most of her life. But any breakdown that landed her in a psych ward would often come with an undifferentiated schizophrenic title too.

Mental illness is a gray cloud inside of a gray cloud. It gets sharpened into focus with different names, but names change, and with that, identities change. She felt like a shape shifter with each new name, hoping, somehow, it could pin her to her right self, and help. The names didn't help. The drugs, as I saw it, just numbed her. Certainly they helped keep her calm and functioning reasonably well throughout her life, but I wonder what went missing under that murk.

But a state hospital would have just kept her drugged and chained to a bed indefinitely. If she had been born a few years earlier, into the previous generation, she would have been lobotomized.

She thought that if she was good and worked hard at getting better they would let her out. They hadn't told her she was going to stay for three years, regardless of her progress. It hurts me to hear her tell this part of the story, that they didn't tell her, didn't think it mattered, or that she wasn't lucid enough or old enough to consult. It would have been better for her if they had told her. All summer and through the fall she worked, was obedient and serious in therapy, listened and gave up her secrets. She wanted to be able to leave for Christmas, a holiday that mattered to her, to be with her family.

November came and her therapist told her she would not be home for Christmas, or any time soon. Enraged, she stormed down the long hall to the sunroom, the only place on the adolescent floor without locked grates on the windows. She kicked the window out, smashing her leg through the glass in its metal frame, and jumped out of the window, four stories to the ground, and broke her leg.

It was pouring rain. She dragged herself along the sidewalk for a little while in a sorry attempt to escape until a doctor found her and carried her back in.

After months of isolation, she started over. Now more jaded, I imagine, but still hopeful about entering the rest of the world again. She finished high school in the hospital and applied for college when she was almost eighteen. They had a classroom right there in the psych ward, with some of the best teachers from the University of Michigan teaching their classes—it was not the worst place to finish high school, really. Her graduating class was eight people, the largest one yet.

How much of this early damage predisposed my mom to Dad's cons? I suspect there is a relationship. But I assign no blame to Mom for being duped.

I found out about this when I was a teenager and I asked her about her prom. I didn't go to my own prom because I thought the whole thing was stupid and I wanted to know what hers was like. I sat numbly as she spilled this whole story out. "So. I didn't go to prom either," she ended.

She left straight from the hospital for college, in 1968, to Grand Valley State, to study psychology. For a year she did wonderfully, was so happy to be in the world, content to have schoolwork. She left college, though, perhaps out of this very confidence. She moved to Israel to work on a kibbutz for a year, a hippie dream of hers, and it was like heaven. The square, yellowy photos I have seen of her from this time seem un-real—cool, free kids playing at utopia, working the earth and forging a tiny community. During the day she picked tomatoes or packed green grapes into crates. On breaks from daily work she killed scorpions and snakes or read sci-fi novels under the pistachio trees. At night she learned to cook and dance and to repair shoes and tires, trying to catch up to the things she missed growing up in a hospital. She had come so far.

When she returned to the States, she moved back to Grand Rapids, but it was impossible to pick up her studies again. One semester in, she was failing all of her classes. A friend of hers advised her not to go back. She thought about what she wanted to do, where she'd like to be, and she decided she wanted to move to Baltimore to be with her Aunt Molly, the woman for whom I was named.

"The first year," she said, "I just shadowed her." Just followed her around, modeling her, learning the adult world. Soon she got a job as an assistant in a home for mentally disabled children, and the reward of it encouraged her to finish her degree in clinical psychology. She went *toward* her own problems with an intense bravery and intelligence that humbles me, even now. She specialized in them, in order to help others.

After twenty years of working in clinics and managing her own private practice, she left it. Addiction counseling, especially, is brutal—full of failure, managing relapses, deaths. She took a job without any intense emotional requirements: in the footwear department at REI. She outfitted adventurers with boots for mountain climbing in Kenya or canoeing the Au Sable River. It was a more pleasant and low-stakes way of continuing on as a therapist of sorts. Not in spite of it all—the betrayal, abuse, deceit—but *because* of it all, she still loved people. She gave them what she could—a little help, a little conversation, some good advice—then set them off.

40

Dad spent some of his seven-year prison term in Milan, Michigan, and the rest in Pennsylvania. I was probably about fifteen when my grandpa took me to visit him. My mom would not take me, and my sister did not want to go; she didn't want to see him there. My grandpa had been trying to strike up an open communication with Dad. He'd been writing him letters, sending him books, hoping to get to the root of his choices, wanting to know *why why why*. Of course, inquiring this of the criminal himself assumes the criminal (1) has a reason and (2) is capable of articulating that reason. I had already given up my faith in these two concepts, but I was—we all were—curious to see what Grandpa could elicit from Dad.

In every way my grandpa was different from my dad. Grandpa was so smart and good, so transparent and open; he liked to ask me about my life and talk about death and

God and art. A Jewish migrant from Russia who fled with his family from their home to escape persecution, my grandpa was a hard worker, a voracious reader, and a deep thinker. He was a Marine, fought in the Philippines in WWII, married his only sweetheart and dedicated himself to her, and made a good, honest living as a salesman. He made a real life all of his family depended on, including me. He looked straight at me when he spoke. He was one of the few people I communicated with on any meaningful level as a teenager.

It was winter, and we drove to Pennsylvania slowly. The night before our visit we went to see a movie in a tiny, empty theater. I can't remember much about it but I am certain it was a disaster movie involving an earthquake or volcano, and I remember watching the actors running while computer-generated lava oozed over the streets of their town. I remember crying a little at that in the dark cold of the theater, wishing that would happen. I was in high school now, and I wasn't seeing a therapist anymore, nor was I talking much to anyone. The appeal of total annihilation as a viable alternative to my current existence didn't seem worrisome to me. Inwardly, I was as miserable as a teen could be. Outwardly, I was fine, didn't care, didn't care about anything.

Over dinner that night at a Denny's near our hotel Grandpa tried to draw me out. "Molly," he started, "are you angry at your father?"

I stopped poking at my food to look at him. He was smiling, patient. "No. Well. I mean, I am angry about what he did to my sister."

". . . but you're not angry about what he did to *you*? He did this to you, also, Molly, not just your sister. You talk like he's only your sister's father."

I drew my arms in. "No, because I already didn't care about him. She cared. He was her world. He was never my world. He was nothing to me."

We let this utterance sit between us, both feeling how false it was. I regretted saying it, and felt old in that moment, too old for myself. "You know, Molly, you are allowed to be angry. He is your father. He abandoned you."

I looked at Grandpa: his kind brown eyes, his gentle smile radiating calm love. I wished so much he was my dad instead. I was jealous of my mom that she'd had him for a father—wise, understanding, caring, strong. I didn't know at the time he'd failed to protect her, too.

"No," I said, trembling, tears in my eyes. Just no. That's all I could manage. We left the conversation at the table and returned to the hotel in silence.

The next day we pulled up to the prison, a long, low building, surrounded by fields of unmarred snow in all directions. Official as school. We filled out the forms, passed through the metal detector and into the visiting room.

Up until that point I thought the room would be like it was in the movies—telephone stations with plexiglass partitions that mournful wives would press their palms to melodramatically. But this was not maximum security. Instead it was open, with long lunch tables with fixed stools exactly like the ones in the school cafeteria.

I looked into the faces of the prisoners around the room, trying to recognize one of them. Some of them were sharing snack cakes or chips from the near-empty vending machine in the corner. The visitors were smiling and talking softly, with an uncanny pleasant sadness, as if today were some tragic holiday. Grandpa held my hand and pulled me toward an empty table, where we sat to wait for Dad to come out.

He seemed so short and small, like a boy, when I saw him in his jumpsuit. He smiled and asked Grandpa about the trip, the weather, and they talked about adult things while I watched their faces quietly.

Dad was talking about us girls now, as if I weren't there. He didn't look at my eyes, even when he did turn to talk to me.

"Hi Dad," I remember saying, as if I had been invisible during the entire first half of the conversation. I kept a smile on as he asked me general questions about my life, like nothing at all was wrong, like we weren't in a prison but at home, on the couch.

When all of his questions about who was in what grade and who liked what subjects and who better not be dating yet were answered, Dad sighed heavily and said nothing for a while. Grandpa brought a paperback book out of his leather coat pocket and handed it to Dad, who turned it over calmly to the guard who'd rushed over to inspect it. The guard took the book back to his station and passed some small electronic device over it and then returned it, a little annoyed. Grandpa was holding back, I could tell. It was supposed to be just a nice visit, nothing too serious, I reasoned. Soon we ran out of unimportant things to say.

"If I did it, it was an out-of-body experience," I heard Dad say when Grandpa asked him what he thought about the crimes. The sentence sank on us. All three of us looked at the floor. No one said anything else after that.

The sunny photomural of a woodland scene on the wall I had been glancing at all during the visit, I learned, was a backdrop for photos. An inmate squeezed hard the two young boys he was having his picture taken with, and they laughed and squealed in mock pain. It was heartbreaking to me, the photomural, that fake forest. I watched the other kids line up with their dads for photos. Very young kids seemed happy, oblivious, but the older kids were sad. I watched their eyes when the camera flashed. Their inmate dads smiled proudly. The kids were hurt, under their smiles. I looked at my grandpa and my dad and thought about myself. I was hurt too, I decided. I wanted to scream it to both of them, to the whole prison. Instead, I smiled, and put on my coat, and hugged Dad goodbye.

Outside, we walked back to the car, along a perfectly shoveled path scattered with salt grinding underfoot. For sure, I thought, that would be the last time I'd ever do that. He'd get out of prison, and this part of my life would be over, and I'd never have to visit my dad in prison ever again. Before we split paths to either side of the car I turned and hugged my grandpa hard without saying anything.

41

Most people who go to prison, about 90 percent, get out. Consider that for a moment.

If it's true that most people get out, what kind of place should prison be? It shouldn't be a machine that people pass through and come out *worse* on the other side. Ideally, it should be a place that teaches you how to never return there.

And when your loved one is in there, you are so certain he is learning this lesson. He says he is learning this lesson. He appears to be learning this lesson. I can't speak for other people's experience with prisons, but I can tell you that this lesson was lost on my dad.

In my favorite childhood movie, *The Point*, an animated hippie hero's journey from the seventies, featuring a soundtrack by Harry Nilsson that my mom pressed on to us, the pivotal scene of the main character's banishment to the wilderness never elicited the correct emotion in me. The boy is banished from his pointed town, in which everything has a literal and metaphorical "point," because he has a round head, no point. Of course the wild world outside of the pointed town is rich and interesting and of course at the end he returns to the pointed town wise and triumphant, which causes, for some reason, everything there to lose its point. It seemed obvious that for this freak, this round-headed boy, being banished from his hometown of pointed people and pointed things ought to be taken as a reward not a punishment. Why was exile always framed as a punishment? Not only did the boy get to escape all of those horribly judgmental people, he became *activated* in banishment—challenged, strengthened, enlightened.

The message, as it always is presented, is that banishing a transgressor for some grave wrongdoing—sending him to prison—is the worst punishment short of death. The message is crucially prosocial in a culture that thrives on regulated cooperation. It didn't resonate with me because I already felt alone, I suppose, and some kind of formal release would have seemed like a blessing. How I felt staying on the Amish farm. Living on the other end of this, though, as a person left behind by someone banished to prison, I started to see another angle.

Typical social connections to family, friends, coworkers, even strangers, which keep an average person afloat, have some other purpose for the sociopath. Not some other purpose, rather the same purpose—just intensified one thousandfold. Instead of benefiting from mutual respect and concern, always with an eye toward fairness and responsibility, the sociopath takes from the network but doesn't give. He cheats.

And the cheater relies, fundamentally, on the honesty of everyone else. He skates over these networks to dissemble, manipulate, or to just take whatever benefits him. His rewards, at no cost, are enormous. His receiving these rewards is especially painful for noncheaters to observe. It makes sense that there is not only formal punishment for cheating, but social shaming as well, which can be a hugely powerful motivator against cheating.

In prison, the cheater has no access to his quarry. In theory. The theory fails when the quarry is his family.

42

"MOLLY."

The secretary hollered my name from within the glass cube of the principal's office waiting room, out into the hall where I was sitting between one boy with a bleeding nose and another boy with a DIY tattoo of half a smiley face he'd just punctured into himself in the bathroom with a safety pin and Bic pen.

Moving from middle school to high school, I'd transferred from regular visits with the school counselor to regular visits with the principal. She looked up at me from over her glasses when I entered her office, then looked back down, and remained looking at the papers on her desk or writing while she spoke to me.

"Mrs. Higgs says you were doing needlepoint in AP English instead of participating and you refused to put it away when she asked you to."

"Yup. A tableau. Vase of hydrangeas," I said. I gave it to Mrs. Higgs at the end of the year. The principal remained stoic, writing something on a notepad.

"Explain that to me."

"She's making us read *Jurassic Park*. *Jurassic Park?* It pisses me off that she thinks this is AP English material. I even asked her if I could read something else, and she said no, so whatever. I tried."

The principal looked up to glance at the book I held in my lap. *The Revolt of the Masses,* by José Ortega y Gasset. She sighed heavily. "Have you ever read the *Tao Te Ching?*"

I shook my head. "It's in the library. Where you always are." I nodded. "Don't forget that you are in *high school*, Molly." I laughed with some disdain. She continued, "If you want to get through this, you've got to go with the flow. For now. It will be easier on you, and hopefully I'll see less of you in here."

The advice disheartened me, as advice to "just give in" always does when offered to young idealists. "You have to go to gym class, you have to read *Jurassic Park*, you have to stop correcting the grammar in Mr. Kasprzak's study guides, you have to *stop* working ahead in your Chem I book so that you'll have to *start* paying attention to lectures and *stop* getting sent down here for writing *poetry* during class."

I am certain I rolled my eyes. "Or I will have to call your parents in here," she added.

"Yeah, you go ahead and do that. Please do that."

I meant it sarcastically at the time, but see how much I meant it.

I don't think my teachers knew I loved them. I just wanted them to do better. I wanted to test them because I couldn't test my own parents, a mundane emotional drama enacted in high schools as often as any other. I turned to testing myself in the library, tearing through the poetry section, then the odd names in fiction: Dostoyevsky, Tolstoy, Chekhov. In my head I slowly practiced the syllables of their names in case I was ever asked what I spent all of my time doing.

I didn't get the chance to say their names out loud, nor did I get to hear anyone else speak them, not for years anyway. I didn't talk to anyone about what I was reading or writing. Then I stopped reading novels. Too many families in novels.

I didn't like to see people caring about their families, or insisting that their private family story should be meaningful to others. I'd given up on books and movies in which any character primarily concerned him or herself with wistfulness or anger or adoration or fear or envy or desire or disgust or regret or bitterness or plain love toward a brother or sister or mother or father. I hated stories of wonderful mothers or fathers especially.

And regular stories couldn't fool me anymore. I felt their falseness. Their rounded, finite arcs, tidy rise and fall, buttressing values, their little lessons, like solved equations. Insulting. I'd look up from a book, or away from a movie, and see the world again—its mutant patchwork, invalid formulas, no arcs—and feel akin. I started to read only nonfiction: honest history, deep science. Plain subjects, but not understood. At home in tangles of chemistry formulas, mute images of anatomy, senselessness, the empty action of animals, clouds, the plates of earth shifting. The bloodless categorization of geology textbooks: metamorphic, sedimentary, igneous. The textbooks trusted me to learn the names of everything and to fix the equations. I loved them for that. I didn't love what stories asked me to do: to join, to hope, to trust. Those books, the novels, felt like propaganda.

I fossilized my idea of family with cold logic, and left it. At some point in my high school reading life I told myself that my family members were just people I happened to be related to, nothing more. It was utterly random that I emerged from this lineage and not another—my appearance among these particular people didn't mean anything special, and whatever bonds of affection existed among us were forged merely out of a combination of obligation, hormonal chemistry, and an unthinking survival imperative. I didn't choose them and they didn't choose me, so it couldn't be love. I left love *as a concept* and moved toward anything else—science, philosophy, art.

I just wanted something genuine, some real ideas, some challenge; I wanted to read the opposite advice the principal had given to me: *don't go with the flow, don't give in, reach.* The library did not, in fact, have the *Tao Te Ching,* so I drifted to the philosophy section and picked the shortest book I could find: *Ecce Homo* by Nietzsche.

Without any real understanding of this man's story or what he'd written before, the book ruffled me open with how bleakly *funny* it was. I didn't know books could be like that, alternately insightful and proudly psychotic, loose with ingratitude toward his whole field and most of his influences, Socrates to Schopenhauer. The ridicule of chapter titles alone ("Why I Am So Wise," "Why I Am So Clever," "Why I Write Such Good Books") jolted me into a private adoration for black, very black humor, intentional or not (I hadn't yet learned about his reported descent into madness, during which this book was written). I clearly saw the parody: skewering the egocentric genre of the memoir, which, as far as I could tell, allowed entrance only to those who'd suffered some preciously interesting trauma and survived inexplicably only to inflict on the rest of us smug and simplistic platitudes from their hard-won moralism; or those who'd achieved something grand, like becoming vice president, often just out of luck, selfishness, and privilege dressed to look like honest hard work.

From there I read more Nietzsche, then Plato, Kant, Kierkegaard, whatever philosophy they had, slowly reading, then rereading the chapters with a dictionary on my left, but without context I often settled on the spells the sounds made alone, their strangeness and patter, like chew-songs on my brain.

And I started writing more in my journal, not just reporting the facts of my days but processing them as my own. I wrote about the books I read, one notebook dedicated just to *Moby Dick*, for example; and I wrote about my teachers, about my mom and sister, about painting and drawing, about crushes, friends, bullies, dreams, plain days, weather, and the landscape. I filled a dozen notebooks with reflective writing just in the last two years of high school. I wrote poems too, drew comics, made zines, made art. But it was the journals, the nonfiction, where I felt best about writing; after all, in nonfiction I was only *co*author, I was witness, articulator—the world itself the other author with whom I collaborated.

It was to no one, for no one. I threw each completed journal into a large plastic bin, sealed it, and shoved it back under the bed. I was terrified that they might be read. I was certainly afraid of finally having to admit that I had been a person who lived and knew things.

At the end of high school I gave up my science track and veered off to an art school on the other side of the country. After graduating high school without much fanfare, I left immediately, alone, and with joy.

43

"It would be the most extreme sign of vulgarity to be related to one's parents."
—Friedrich Nietzsche, *Ecce Homo*

44

Early in college I shoplifted. This is hard for me to say. It didn't start how it starts with some kids, as a dare among friends, or as a way of getting high or proving something; I was alone in it. It started as it started when I first stole that book of baby names in the aisle at Kroger: out of unresolvable desire.

It was a sterling silver mood ring, the next first thing. I was holding it in my hand on the way to the cashier in this little boutique and I realized it was either the ring or dinner with friends at Denny's later, where we'd hang out and eat cheap sandwiches and drink coffee. I wanted both so bad. I liked the idea of the mood ring, what a novelty: *this will tell me how I am*, I thought, examining it in the tray. I was fifteen, working in a kitchen, and spending my money on my own phone line at home and whatever food or CDs I bought for myself. Dad was in jail by this time. *This will tell me how I am.*

I just held it in my hand and walked out. Later, as I became more serious about stealing in college, I felt so bad about this time, stealing from an independent boutique in my hometown. I suppose I felt more justified stealing from the corporate places at the mall, so I allowed myself to continue.

I stole for financial reasons, on the surface anyway. It was just a few years, this phase. I know it was childish greed. On eBay I'd sell mostly clothes, designer dresses, cashmere sweaters, popular brands, whatever was easy, and besides the small seller's fees it was pure profit, a small hobby, not a career, and nothing I wanted to look too hard at, because, *how ridiculous*, could I really be that ridiculous? My dad is apparently a sociopathic criminal. And myself? What was it about this passionless, calculated theft I could convince myself to perform? What did this make me?

I was careful and certain about it. I'd go to the mall or nicer department stores dressed up to look older and richer, usually a black dress or suit, nice shoes, big businessy purse. The jacket over my arm had two purposes—one was for stealing small items in hand, easy to make disappear under the jacket, in my palm but under the jacket, with fingers over the edge so it looked natural. Its other purpose was to have an easy pocket in which to keep my tools. Each tool had a different purpose for different security devices. First a small pair of scissors, nose-hair trimmers really, the kind with rounded tips so fabrics couldn't get poked or snagged. Those are simply for cutting off the sewn-in sensors some stores use.

The other two items are more serious, felt more intense and evil to have; both were used to remove two different types of plastic security sensors. The first is a small hook, just a thin curve of metal with a flat end and a groove along its length. This removes the most common kind of sensor, the plastic rectangle with a bulge near the end where the pin connects through the clothing. There's a little hole in the top edge of those sensors, made just for this hook, to remove it in case the electromagnet under the counter at the registers fails. The hook slides in and the sensor comes apart, instantly, soundlessly. You can buy these hooks online for about ten dollars.

The third item is a small stack of cylindrical neodymium magnets, rare earth magnets. The smaller pin-and-tab security sensors and the large dome-shaped ones simply pull apart with the magnets placed around them. The magnets are incredibly strong, but brittle and easily break if they snap back together too quickly. They are difficult to work with for this reason. Pinches and blood blisters covered my fingers when I first tried these. They are sold online, mostly for scientific experiments, toys, wind turbines, hard drives, magnet motors, audio speakers, stop-motion animation, and fishing-reel brakes. I often wondered if anyone ever saw the corner of my jacket strangely attached to a metal fixture or a car I passed by too closely, as occasionally happened, and my yanking it away with pretend calm. All of these tools stuck together in a weird clump because of the magnets, and seemed more evil for it.

Of course, I had to use these tools in the dressing room. I knew which stores had unattended dressing rooms, or didn't count your items on the way in, or if they did, which ones didn't count them on the way out. Most stores do not count your items on the way out, and the nicest shops do not count your items at all. I knew to go during the busiest hours on the weekends, when salespeople were distracted, rushed, or focused on their regulars, not paying much attention to what I had in my arms. If one of them noticed one of my items, suggesting something to go with it or complimenting it somehow ("Oh that is *just* your color!"), I'd put it back. If they asked me if I was ready for a room I'd say yes, even if I wasn't, because I didn't want them to take the items from me and see for certain what I had. Mostly the people working in retail simply don't care enough, or get paid enough, to worry about shoplifters. I was quiet in the dressing room, zipping and unzipping my huge bag with my finger behind the zipper to silence it, rolling up $300 cashmere sweaters with the tags tucked in neatly, without damage. I was friendly but neutral to the salespeople, smiling, in no hurry. I'd bring dummy items in with me, just to have something to leave behind. Once removed, I'd hide the sensors behind the mirror, or on the top of the partition between rooms, or simply attach them to some item I'd leave behind. I'd steal the hangers too. I didn't want them to know, even when I was already gone, that anything had been stolen.

I saw security guards or mall cops following the wrong people. Sometimes I saw other shoplifters. I mean, I saw the bad ones. They were young girls mostly, and they'd be carrying overloaded shopping bags—an obvious sign they'd been added to, since salespeople are taught to use multiple bags for big purchases instead of stuffing one bag full. Also the girls would look around, making eye contact with everyone, which real shoppers don't do. They'd sometimes even be looking straight up, nervously checking for cameras. They looked plainly sneaky, worried.

The color of my skin protected me from suspicion, I know. This makes me feel sick.

Being a successful shoplifter is not about pretending to be fine; it's about being fine. You must convince yourself first. It is hard in the beginning because it feels evil. But then, it's not like lying at all. This is how people change anyway, in any direction, good or bad: I'm going to be the person who doesn't smoke anymore, I'm going to be the person who writes poetry now, I'm going to be the person who trusts this person. I'm going to be the person who isn't shoplifting. You transform yourself all the time, and a new self sticks if you keep choosing it.

I was calm, bored looking. Shoppers have that dreamy drift, especially women, especially in nice clothing stores. I drifted with them, focused on the clothes. I didn't look around nervously, I didn't hesitate or hurry out afterward, didn't act like anything was wrong. After a while, this was no act. I was just shopping, absorbed. I felt utterly safe, at ease, like everyone else.

I didn't think about my dad at the time, but I do now. I'm saying this because I know what it's like to make the wrong choice, over and over, as if taunting the consequences, practically asking them to come straighten you up.

And to act secretly, build a whole small, bad world in private, like an invisible dimension running just under the one everyone else lives in.

You prop up a better self to your loved ones. A dummy self that is you, really, the you they love, but without the evil element. Exactly how theft works. That cover, that safe self who appears to be shopping honestly and not stealing, you realize, must now come home, make her boyfriend dinner, do her homework, go to work, be a gracious daughter, *keep it up*.

The distance Dad placed between himself and every regular person, all of us, made sense to me when I saw it from the inside. It was a residue, I suppose, that builds, this safety in distance, to keep loved ones *especially* away from the truth. Protection. Which is a kind of love. And also a margin for his actions, a pivot point upon which his selves could turn.

I knew enough to stop. I did think of myself as different from my friends and almost everyone else I knew. There was a stain on me. A lack of trust in honest methods. It came out of something beyond him—beyond us both, as thieves—a little corner we didn't keep clean enough.

I often thought about his crimes and decided he could have gotten away without being caught if he had just stopped sooner. Perhaps just not done the very last one, the eleventh robbery, and everything would have been different. It is hard to stop when things are going well. Criminals get greedy. Maybe you need a reason to stop: a fear, a little imagination for the future, your future, your family's future.

I didn't think shoplifting was good or cool, or that it was vigilante justice against the fashion industry or big corporations. It was simply a way to make money when I had none. To me, high-end clothing stores were perfectly ridiculous. The thick, clean mood of luxury, pinched offerings, blind admiration of the shoppers, how they smelled like empty want, wanting to look more beautiful, more happy: they all seemed like suckers. I didn't see what they saw in the stuff. I didn't get the people who bought the clothes from me on eBay, new with tags, for near-retail price; I didn't feel how they felt about these pieces of fabric.

I didn't enjoy the thrill of it; I hated the thrill, hated walking through the doors expecting an alarm but knowing it wouldn't come. When I had extra money I would stop, for months even, and never think about it. I didn't justify it to myself. I didn't brag or tell anyone about it. My boyfriend in college certainly knew what was happening; with clothes and money appearing weekly it would've been hard to miss. He'd confront me, remind me of how horrible it would be to get caught, tell me this was the last time and to never do it again. I'd agree and get better at hiding it from him. Over a couple years I made thousands of dollars doing this. The money went to car repairs, medical bills, trips home, rent, practical things. I was never caught, never came even close to being caught.

I felt guilty. I could block the guilt, though.

Then the upscale department store I'd frequently milk installed a security guard just inside their doors. The steady shrinkage had become apparent to them, I could see. I'd nod and smile at the security guard on the way out, like all the other tidy white women did, and he'd sleepily nod back. I felt a little sick with this exchange, and maybe a little triumphant.

And then, I just stopped.

I want to say I took a hard look at myself or found some moral or mystical reason compelling me to mend my ways. But honestly, I just wanted to get away with it, as he hadn't.

I knew it would be only a matter of time until I made a mistake or got sloppy with my methods and found myself with a criminal record, even if just a misdemeanor. I resolved to quit while I was ahead. Now, here's where I did have something to prove.

It was a way of acting through—then resolving—the pattern of theft that destroyed my family. I see that now.

I was lucky, so lucky I got to play this out. Maybe I was lucky, too, that I wasn't predisposed in some way to become addicted to stealing. Maybe I wanted to prove that you couldn't become addicted to stealing.

I lived without the extra padding in my bank account and felt fine about it. After all, I didn't crave it. I just had to adjust my spending. Then, I didn't miss it. Even now I still see kids stealing in stores all the time, and I start to feel nervous suddenly, like it exposes me by just being around it. A lifelong nervousness around stealing: I think of this as fair, at least something close to fair, as a punishment.

45

It's a little sociopathic. This conscious break with reality I am describing in the method of stealing, I know it is sociopathic. I can explain what it feels like when it happens.

Your plan numbs you. You focus on the plan. You know if the plan goes well, you'll be pleased afterward, but you are not pleased in the execution of it. There is no pleasure, no feeling at all. It *is*, Dad, a little like an out-of-body experience.

Except that it's more of an out-of-morals experience. A purposeful stepping out of them. That's the difference, Dad. There's no helplessness involved, at all.

You feel gross. But you choose to not stop. You have all the time in the world to stop! You have a million chances to not go through with it. But you do. It's like you're on the other side of yourself now.

46

What does it mean to take care of someone? To protect? What parents do, with such good intentions, hiding all the bad bits, scrubbing their kids' intake of information from the Internet, TV, friends, school, books, even from their own adult lives, as much as possible, padding their kids into a nicer, safer, false version of the world? An utter betrayal of truth? What parent does not do this? Only cruel ones.

47

Dad got out when I was twenty-one. He served seven years of a ten-year sentence. Thanks to the United Auto Workers he got his old job back, which I know seems insane to anyone who doesn't know unions like the UAW. One of his brothers took him in at first, helping him with money and other essentials, like a kid moving back in after college.

It was Thanksgiving and I was on break from the Savannah College of Art and Design, back in Michigan for a visit. Dad's brother, Casimir, was hosting a subdued release party at his new house. My sister and I drove there together. She seemed happy, a little jittery, like me. The house was in a new development, gleaming concrete driveways and fresh sod, the house still so clean. We walked through the door and I remember standing in the vestibule looking across the room to my dad, flanked by his two brothers, all with beers in their hands, laughing intensely. I heard him making a joke about having to sleep on a potato sack in prison. His brothers laughed hard and slapped him on the shoulders. The air in the room was bright and vivid, like Christmas, and people seemed genuinely happy.

I didn't want to see him. How much easier it would have been to just lose him forever. Now he was here drinking a Corona and it was how it had always been, and he seemed so happy, it was worth it to hide my feelings for him, for his party.

The first time I met with my father by myself when he was out of jail I met him at a Big Boy restaurant. The same one where I first saw him lie to me, saw it plainly. A friendly but crappy diner, with exposed brick inside and giant gumball machines in the vestibule. The breakfast buffet was still out, rubbery eggs and gray sausages steaming steadily in their pans, a geriatric calm.

He was sitting at a booth already; he rose and hugged me hard and patted my back. We sat across from each other and read our menus. He was always bad at making eye contact, and now it seemed worse. He looked out of the window while he spoke. If we locked eyes for more than a few seconds he would flutter his lids and look away. He told me he was excited to eat Big Boy's signature sandwich again, the Slim Jim; this was his favorite sandwich and he had been looking forward to it. I asked him about the food in jail. He said the holiday meals were nice, but he'd save up his money so he could buy treats in the jail store like ice cream and nicer sandwiches. I looked over the giant menu of American food, embarrassed by its glut.

He asked me about my life and my plans and kept the conversation fast and light, not seeming to register much about my answers. He had that way of asking about things that parents sometimes have that sounds inherently, although probably not intentionally, dismissive, "You still, uh, with that *guy*? What was his name?" No, I wasn't, I was dating someone new now. He'd run his hand through his graying hair, purse his lips, and study a brick or the saltshaker intently. "You gotta get the school thing straightened out. On the right track. What were you doing? Illu*stra*tion? It's good you quit that," and then his strange slow laugh that sounded fake always, like a mask of a laugh. I wanted to be casual and fine, as he was, but I felt like concrete, and I wanted to talk about my real questions. I could feel them peering out of me. I kept quiet.

And then, he lived a normal life. He bought a house with my sister, using his money but her credit (his was ruined, of course), and a car and found a new girlfriend, a woman he could go dancing with and take care of, but someone he didn't talk to much. We found out later he never told her about the robberies or the prison term.

He worked overtime, as much as he could, and he bought things; he even bought me a used car. A year after that meeting at Big Boy I had dropped out of SCAD because I couldn't afford rent after a year as a full-time student working nearly full-time in low-wage jobs and I couldn't take out any more loans, so I came back to Michigan and took a steady job at the College for Creative Studies downtown, trying to finish school part-time at Wayne State. He would come visit me sometimes, during the middle of the day, just to say something, usually slipping me fifty dollars before leaving. He walked slowly and with great control and pride, how short men sometimes do. I liked his visits but I always felt a strange pang of guilt when I saw him walking up, like I had been caught doing something wrong, or been reminded of something I had forgotten.

Now there were casinos downtown. Before you'd have to go to Windsor, which wasn't such a bad thing, and in fact back then the exchange rate would give you a leg up anyway. But now the casinos were here, and they were so easy. My sister told me he bragged about being able to punch in at work and leave to go play blackjack at the casino. If he wasn't back in time to punch out a coworker would punch out for him. It was routine.

I moved around, into my own places, and transferred to Oakland University in Rochester, the city where I was born. After seven years of working on a bachelor's degree, switching majors and schools more often than was reasonable, I realized I would never be able to work full-time and finish school at OU just because of scheduling conflicts, so I quit my job and moved in with my sister and Dad just so I could graduate. By that time he pretty much lived with his girlfriend, although he always kept some things there in his room. I didn't see him much. Even my sister said he was hard to pin down. Despite this, he was demanding, especially when it came to fulfilling obligations. If there was a Brodak family picnic or wedding, we were expected to be there. I would try to make it but didn't make the efforts my sister made. She seemed badgered by him, unhappy and anxious. He made a good salary but there never seemed to be enough; besides, his retirement was coming up and of course he did not have the savings other men had at this point in their lives.

He had a strange black jewelry box I liked to look in. It was full of old foreign money, some photos of women, unidentifiable teeth, little chains, and rings. All mysteries. My sister said she saw betting slips around but I didn't see them, I never knew what they looked like. I saw stacks of bills sometimes, his neatly penciled block letters showing how much he paid on each one. I saw he was paying restitution to the government for the robberies.

Soon I graduated and moved to an apartment in Ferndale, a suburb just on the north side of 8 Mile Road, across from Detroit proper.

As he neared his retirement age, GM offered him a buyout. He would get $62,000 (a figure he would later minimize in a letter to me) plus a nice pension afterward. He took it. This was how it ended for him.

48

Dad and my sister were OK for a while, back to being a little family. They went to church together, played euchre together at a regular game, went to Red Wings games, and hosted barbeques. I saw them almost as they were before: a sort of unbalanced couple, but happy, choosing each other still, like family does. He could have just gone on like this, retired with a normal life, and with everyone's forgiveness.

But money in his hands was dangerous, especially a large chunk like his retirement buyout. First he had to pay back my sister $20,000. He'd stolen two blank cash advance checks from her credit line that had come in the mail and cashed them both, ten grand each, forging her signature. He told her later, when she got the bill, that it was for an emergency and he'd had no time to ask her. He insisted on saying that he did not "steal" the money from her, only borrowed it. He wouldn't say where the money went, which meant it went to bookies.

He had also stolen her social security number and opened credit cards in her name, but paid them off so she didn't even know until much later. He did it to me too, but only once. I didn't have the spotless credit my sister had, not worth stealing; it was just a gas card with a low limit that I found later on my credit report. Soon he kept asking me for the title to my car, "just to have the paperwork on file." I stalled and stalled; I knew he wanted to pawn the title. I knew it wouldn't have been worth that much, which made it all the more heartbreaking. He must have been desperate. He filed for bankruptcy a few months before the last crime. He was denied. They said he made too much money.

My sister was concerned for him, and I felt her concern. She was stressed again, like she'd been as a child. I felt helpless, but I kept in touch with her, as a listener, a supporter. I suggested she start thinking about the next step in case something happened to him.

"Oh yes," I remember her saying, "I have a secret savings account he doesn't know about." Just like a spouse waiting for the other shoe to drop. She saw him sliding away from normalcy and she'd been arming herself. Myself, I did what I always did when things were bad: keep quiet, watch carefully. I took my sudden stomach pain, which would later be diagnosed as ulcers that still plague me, as a pretty unequivocal sign of some bottled-up anxiety over what was surely coming our way.

He had gambled away all of the money from the buy-out within three months. On the weekends he'd sleep for a few hours at home in the morning, then leave for twenty-four-hour-long stretches at the casino. He'd come home and sleep for a few hours in the morning, then start again. His car was repossessed. He tried to hide it from my sister by telling her that it was in the shop, but eventually she was getting phone calls from bill collectors. Soon from the mortgage company. The money she'd been paying him for "rent" had not been going toward the mortgage; in fact, it was three months behind.

He fought with his girlfriend constantly, shuttling between her house and "his" house to sleep, spending all of his time at work or the casino. My sister knew what was coming. She told him, explicitly, in a straight, plain way I could not imagine myself doing with him, to not commit any crimes. She said "just please don't do anything stupid."

She said he looked at her with extreme hatred at that moment. "Don't tell me about my business," he said. "I am your father."

She told him she would help him if he was just straight with her, and tell her what was going on. Then the anger turned into a dismissive chuckle. He waved her off and left again. My sister would have, and could have, just handed him all the money he needed if he had just told her the truth.

When we were kids, my sister showed me the notes he left her when he'd secretly steal all of her saved-up allowance out of her jewelry box. The money would be replaced by plain slips of paper with "I.O.U." written in large letters and the amount underneath. "$37." "$24." "$88." When he was arrested the first time, he owed her $5,000, all stolen, in secret, out of her jewelry box.

49

Maybe private worlds are all there are. Talking about them is a way of conjuring gravity between them, a way to pull them near and make them matter to each other. I mean, to make any one of them matter at all. Certainly the force of describing them also changes them.

But it can't be better to say nothing.

Everyone lives alone in families. Everyone goes alone into action, love, and work. Sometimes, it's why we work. Everyone goes alone into sickness, too.

50

"Scrub extra hard," the nurse said, "y'aint going bathe again for a while."

She handed me a thin stitch of soap and papery blue booties and a papery blue dress. I shut the door to the cavernous shower stall and scrubbed extra hard.

It was five in the morning, and very dark in surgery intake. I emerged in my paper clothes, calm and flat, used to hospital procedures at that point, without marvel. I set myself onto a bed where I'd stay for the whole summer, headless.

They started in with the IVs, and no matter how much I told each new nurse that my veins are thin and rolly and likely to blow, each new nurse tried it her way until it failed. This time, through a multi-poked failure patch, she found a vein that rolled as soon as she punctured it and a jet of blood spurted from my arm onto the chest of my plus one, my boyfriend at the time, who promptly fainted.

Then I was officially alone. The anesthesiologist came in, chubby and glowing like a movie star, and she told me to start counting back from ten. Cold crept up my arm and then I woke up.

The seven-hour surgery to remove the tumor that had been growing behind my eyes and the small coma afterward, where no one went, especially not me, was not even a *tick-tock*, just a *tick*-and then someone telling me it had happened.

Like when I was told I was losing my vision and I was weirdly lactating because I had a brain tumor, pea-sized, pressing on my optic nerve, growing into my pituitary gland. This two weeks before I'd leave for grad school. Not cancer, just a cellular malfunction, she called it—stubborn cells, stubbornly not disappearing but huddling up. I was told, I was shown. *See there? That bit, you know,* he tapped the MRI image. I saw but did not know.

A cellular malfunction: no purpose, no meaning, no particular intent. When I was told, I saw the Flower Sermon but Buddha holding up not a meaningless wordless flower for no one to understand except Mahākāśyapa, but a small pea-sized, scallop-edged, rubbery tumor. For no one to understand, period.

My mom, my sister, my grandparents, and my then-boyfriend rallied around me when we found out. My grandpa scoured the Internet for reasons why this happened to me, and would call with suggestions: *Birth control pills? Illegal drugs? Pent-up psychic energy? Cell-phone radiation?* There was no reason, the doctor insisted. No reason: the worst reason of all.

Dad heard about it from my sister. It had been about two years since his buyout, and since I'd left for graduate school. I just never saw him anymore; even when I was home visiting, he wasn't around. I know this is no excuse; I could have called him to tell him about my tumor. But I didn't. We didn't talk about it. He didn't call me when he heard about it; he didn't say a word.

Now in my MFA program, I grew my brain tumor in private. I went to class, wrote poems, walked up and down the big West Virginia hills. I lived with my symptoms in se- cret, adapting to tunnel vision, dabbing lactation away on bathroom breaks. I mostly told no one. I was fine. And not. Like most people.

Friends I grew close to would learn the two heavy things: dad bank robber, such an interesting story; brain tumor, in- teresting story, how sad. I had a script for them now and I knew about how long it took to have these conversations. I had a certain way and pace for explaining these things, details managed thoughtfully, calm flat tone meant to deflect pity, the smiles, our mutual amazement, and bright gratitude to prove I did not pity myself. I was fine, I insisted, others had it worse, I was lucky in fact; I was so lucky.

Then exactly midway through my three-year MFA pro- gram at West Virginia University I woke up from surgery.

A bandage sealed over my nostrils, which were stuffed fully with gauze and held open with tiny metal stents. They had cut the bottom connections of my nostrils open a bit to widen the passage for the laser that would enter my sinus, pierce through my skull, and sear the tumor into bits to be removed with a tiny grasping claw. The old Egyptian mummification process—how they'd pull pieces of the brain down through the nose with a hook—that was me; I was the mummy.

Now on the bed I was awake but I was somewhere new in my body. My head was gone. That *I* that lived here had moved down and "I" was in my chest and stomach.

Someone was feeding my missing head small ice chips with a plastic spoon. It struggled with the ice slivers. I wanted to go back to sleep but people kept talking to me, wanting me to eat the ice and nod my head. I could not tell if I was nodding. They wanted me to move my arms. I laughed a little in my guts at their precious concern. *I would be a hero if I moved my arms right now*, I thought, and lifted one arm up to great acclaim. My arm signaled to me via a new route—more direct. Without head-processing. I felt my arm like you'd feel eyes blink. Close up to *self*. Blink now. Feel it? *Right* there. Next to "you." Special, only, brain-self. Imagine that but in your chest.

Time passed in uneven chunks, blurry light or dark rooms where someone else was always in charge of my body and its requirements. I was wheeled down a hallway and I heard the nurses joking about the bald shaved spots on my head, which had been outlined in purple marker. Sensors had been attached there for MRIs before the surgery—*triangulation,* he said; in case they came off, they could be realigned to the markings. "Nice purple rings," I heard them laugh, I heard it through my intestines.

My body was left in the ICU for a while. I was crouched in my stomach. Here's what I did for weeks: I listened.

I couldn't see and I couldn't smell or taste and I couldn't move much to feel anything. I didn't know anything about my head but that it was boarded up in gauze and I didn't live there anymore. But I could hear—all through my body.

I was patient, content to listen, alert and curious about the sounds in the ICU, beeps and groans, wheels wheeling, a phone ringing, a hissing pump, little ticks, gurgling, shoe squeaks if running happened, pad flaps if walking. I listened intently to the sound of someone's lungs being sucked dry of fluid at regular intervals. Words imposed grossly over this. Most patients in the ICU are not in a position to do much talking; it was the nurses who would talk. They arched nets of intimate words over my bed, dumb chatter, cruel things sometimes, disgusting stories about patients, explicit sexual exchanges, evil rants, boring small talk, just regular people at work. They worked around me, a deaf empty body, coldly protecting their own energies from the drain it would be to consider anything more than their patient's physical main-tenance. It was OK; I was busy anyway.

I made games of trying to move each toe or twist my ankles back and forth slowly in regular patterns. I felt the inert power in objecthood, headlessness. It is hard to explain to anyone who hasn't been headless. It's quite freeing. My legs had voices. No: my calves, my ankles, my thighs, my feet all had voices. I lived in them. I saw the world out of my ankles.

What does the world look like out of one's ankles? It looks a little better, honestly.

I felt what I could feel with my hands. I edged my hand inward and felt a thin tube taped where a patch of my pubic hair had been shaved off. My arms were stiff and dead from too many punctures and too much stillness; I could not bend my elbows. After the nurses had run out of normal puncture spots on my arms they had moved onto my hands and fingers and my neck. My arms swelled and bruised over yellow and blue. They were tired. And deeply tired of being me: executing my commands, shoveling food to head, holding and turning and writing and hitting. They lay like soft logs and seemed happy, finally sessile.

Once a nurse sat next to me and talked. Sports, the nice weather I was missing, politics even. I tried hard to nod and smile and make small noises of joy. He then pulled out a foamy white hospitalish ponytail elastic and lifted my head gently with one hand, gathering my disgustingly greasy, dank hair to one side and securing it. "There, I bet that feels better," he said. I instantly flooded with tears, soaking my face bandages. It felt so good, I wanted to tell him. I had never felt anything as good as that. He left and I fell asleep, grateful. I kept that hair band for a while, to remind me.

It was, I don't know, June. I slept, oozed, drooled, and forgot everything about my regular life. I was allowed to exist in this sealed-off space, away from my family, away from even my guilt and anxiety over my family, while my sister remained rooted in the pathway of a freight train.

Then my feeding tube came out. Some bandages came off. Visitors had brought me photos of themselves standing next to the old me, beaming together in the incorrigible safety of normalcy. I saw my mom and my boyfriend looking down on me with uneasy smiles and I knew that look so well. I remembered looking at my mom in a hospital bed after another suicide attempt. I could now see my own small face laboring to smile at her. I had to look away from my visitors. My vision gradually sharpened. But it was remote, like backward through a telescope. I was in no way connected to the information my eyes were now gathering. Trays of real food were delivered to me like jokes.

I turned the head to look at them—the hard fried chicken piece and roll and wet green beans—and honestly thought it was a joke. The trays would eventually be removed, replaced with new ones when I was left alone. My mom had come to West Virginia now to help and she'd spoon broth into me, or my boyfriend would when he could get away from work. Otherwise that was that. Chewing endeavors ceased when my boyfriend noticed I had chewed straight through a small part of my tongue in attempting to eat some bread he'd given me.

I was to be moved out of ICU into a regular room. A physical therapist came to move my limbs. She lifted my legs and bent them at the knee repeatedly, in a goofy staged kick, then cheerily moved on to my sore arms. I groaned to let her know it hurt, surprised at the sound. "You really need some pillows under your arms!" she said, pronouncing "pillows" as "pillers" in the Appalachian style. The catheter came out. I'd have to start walking to the bathroom. "You are young and healthy," my neurosurgeon said when he came to visit me. "Others have it much worse. You should be walking." My morphine button was taken away while I was asleep.

The wires to my head were waking up. I would be lying if I said I was happy to have my head back.

Pain cleans out worry. It puts you in this second, then the next second, and nowhere else. I know it can make you *act* mean, but only heads can *be* mean. I was lucky. I felt rich from decapitation. More advantaged than those still attached to that awful organ. I wasn't wondering *why, why, why* anymore, *what did I do, how did I grow this tumor, how can I be OK now, will it grow back, it will probably grow back, what what what.* Just quietness. Sunk into a ground, a bed, as I had sometimes dreamed, in real liminality now, meshed into a hard space, but not exactly anywhere.

This coming from the kind of person who had lived, as introverted writers and readers do, almost exclusively in her head, regarding her body largely as an irritating, irrational corporation that demanded constant and utterly unappreciated maintenance. The original me would have much preferred bodilessness, and in luck of all lucks here I was with headlessness instead.

In the regular room a woman was wheeled in who at first just groaned horribly or slept. Eventually I saw her up and about, an enormous stretch of stitching up one of her legs and running across her scalp. Once she approached my bed and pointed at her scars. "They was looking for the clot!" She said, "God works in mysterious ways!" She said that a lot, annoyingly. Mostly she said that. She'd say it when she woke up. She'd say it when I'd throw up on myself from the meds. I'd lie there with hot vomit on my chest, pulling steadily on the nurse cord, mad. "God works in mysterious ways," she'd whisper under her breath. She got better, then started asking the nurses for cigarettes and was gone soon after that.

And then I missed her saying it. I said it to myself sometimes. I didn't believe in God exactly, so it became more of a *no one works in mysterious ways; no one works in no ways* after a barf or a pain. It was kind of a constructive *fuck you*. Especially to *knowing*, which had enormously left me. Whereas before I lived in absolute horror of the thing, of the pain, of the meaningless cellular malfunction my brain was bashing against, then it was not the pain or the horror or the malfunction that stopped existing, but my higher-order brain, the very instigator of rotten interpretations of meaningless things.

I started walking. I went outdoors even. My boyfriend helped me outside onto the sad patio. He bought me a lime slush and I sat in the fresh summer afternoon, feeling clean air finally on my gross skin, watching sparrows picking at crumbs, feeling a throb growing in my head.

I almost always dreamed about wading waist-high in Lake Superior until I came to a river of darker water. On the other side of the river was another lake, just as transparent and deep as my lake. From a slant I could see shipwrecks at the bottom of the other lake. I'd stand before the river border between the two lakes, looking but not crossing.

51

I was released from the hospital without a cellular malfunction and with instructions to check regularly under my nose for any clear watery fluid and return immediately if any was detected. "It would be your spinal fluid leaking out of your nose," the nurse said flatly. Because of the stitching in my sinuses I would not be able to bite or chew much, nor lie flat in bed, nor tilt my head forward farther than a few degrees. I was told to not blow my nose for at least six months. I was told that if I sneezed I should return immediately to the hospital.

Mom came to stay. She slept on an air mattress in my office. She spent her time making soft food for me, going for walks in the lovely hills around our house, or talking to me. I felt guilty for her efforts, as much as ever, how I had hated to be picked up or carried as a child, even for fun, because of the strain I felt in her body and how burdensome it made me feel, how being *carried* made me feel *worthless*.

Sewn back on now, my head rethroned itself as tyrant. I remained in bed, mostly watching TV with vague interest. I was too tired and distracted to read, and besides I couldn't hold my arms up very long at the angle I needed to in order to read a book, perfectly level to my exhausting head. If I looked down I felt a flood of hot pain behind my eyes. My head wanted and complained and schemed and envied and nagged and hurt and hurt and hurt. My body went silent. My boyfriend washed me in the tub like a baby. The summer went on like this.

Feeling much as I did after my return from the Amish farm, I soberly rejoined my old life with some resistance. I don't want to seem ungrateful for having to return to "normal" after surviving brain surgery unscathed, or as if I liked being sick because of the attention and care it drew—no, no. Rather, being so thoroughly removed from my life in these safe ways—the farm, the hospital—afforded me a rare chance to reunite with it clear eyed and rejoin it with more compassion for myself and more warmth toward my family. But I failed to stop being a fool, given the chance. I knew the opportunity to reposition myself was wasted on me.

My sister called at the end of the recovery period to check up on me. "Dad's coming to see you," she said.

"No. No thanks. Tell him no. I'm OK."

"Well, he left yesterday. Sorry."

Later that day he walked into the bedroom holding a half-melted cup of chocolate ice cream out in front of him like a torch.

I ate some of it for him. I put the stuff into my head. My head knew the routine. It could smile now and talk pleasantly, pretend to be fine, even better than before.

Dad pulled up the chair, but not too close, chatting a bit about things, being funny and light, gentle, teasing me about the shaved spots on my head. His girlfriend said hello but hung even farther back. He was uncomfortable, I could tell. He was quieter, paused with uncertainty, looked away from me. But he seemed to be honestly trying. My head saw him feeling bad and knew that I must have looked bad. Gross and sick. I wanted to cut my head off.

They stayed about twenty minutes and left, driving the seven hours immediately back to Michigan. I cried some, for my ugly head, knowing itself, and slept like that, with wet face bandages, swollen and sweaty, propped up straight in bed. That was the last time I saw him before he was arrested again.

52

Once, I should admit, once there was one poem I wrote directly about him. In a push of sudden clarity through the dream nonsense I was writing during the first year of my MFA, I wrote a breathless litany of dark facts about Dad, and Mom, and me, bubbling out like confessional foam on three pages or more. I brought the thing to workshop, just, I think, as a test.

The woman with long gray hair who wore hippie batik-print fabric from her wide waist to the ground, and who never forgave me for calling her out on implanting a totally wrong breed of tree frog in her poem about Michigan, was eager to start. "I just don't *like* this," she said with palms upturned, pleading sort of, her head turning in sweeps across our huge table for support. Stiff comments about tone or believability trickled in, punctuated with nods and directive questions from our professor, a poet who knew me well. I sunk down, unusually tense in the shy and flat workshop routine of first-semester grad students.

The wrong-tree-frog woman finally burst. "Even if it were plausible, so what? This poem is just *poor poor me*, my poor sad life, blah, blah—"

Our professor tried to jump in, "Well, let's not—"

"I mean, come on," she said, shaking her head at me, "It's a pity party."

53

Pity party, I'd say to myself, if I ever felt that bubbling again. *Pity party, pity party!* I hear it now.

54

My sister and my dad lived together for seven years after he was released. Seven years in prison, then seven years with her. Their yard had huge cottonwood trees that blew blankets of puffs over everything in the spring. On weekends, dad would shoot squirrels with a pellet gun he kept in the garage. He said he didn't like the nests the squirrels built in his trees, said the ugly clumps ruined the way the trees looked. The nests were too far up to remove so this was the only solution. One evening I walked alone around the perimeter of the yard, just to feel grass under my feet, and found a large pile of small dark bones in his leaf-burning pit.

55

In the last house we lived in together as a family, Dad kept a small chalkboard by the back door. It had pegs bent into crooks for unused keys, and one curved groove on the ledge to keep chalk.

It was Dad's board, not Mom's. He wrote dates on it and other notes or figures that I never understood. They were probably dates of games to watch or plans for ideal times to bet. The chalk was rich and thick, or the board was cheap, so it never erased well. He'd just smear the words and numbers so they looked far away, or underneath black water. Ghost marks would build behind new ones, coding new numbers and words in garble. Some months later it would get washed with a wet towel finally, and it'd look crystal-clear black, like a space instead of a surface.

A blackboard is a chance to say something, make yourself known. It is blankness, like an open door. My dad had a chalkboard. Later, I'd find the Amish dad had one too, and the only chalk for it was kept in his breast pocket. A chalkboard was a space that heard only the voices of the powerful, I learned.

When I was alone I'd choose a nub of chalk and draw a bony flower in the corner of the board, or write "hi!"

Later I'd rush back to erase it, worried that Dad had seen it or worried that he hadn't seen it, I couldn't decide. I'd smear it with my finger, fogging the powder marks down into the black.

Now most of the college classrooms I teach in are out-fitted in whiteboards. They feel greasy, shiny, and depthless, like cheap toys, sharp with the stink of markers. I had imag-ined touching chalkboards with my powdery fingers as a key element in the privilege of teaching.

As a kid in school I'd squint my eyes at the blackboards and imagine them as deep black or green holes, the chalk words floating as if across a tunnel. I'd snap to attention if the teacher called for someone to write an answer or solve a problem on the board.

Up close the board absorbed me. I'd watch its touch point intimately, the chalk on the board wisping off a ground white dust as it went that'd catch on my sweater sleeve, affec-tionately, I believed. Once in a sleepy, first-hour math class I caught my own reflection in the early black of the low windows and froze. It was *me* writing on the board. I didn't recognize my own handwriting on the board when I sat back down. But I had seen myself with the chalk in my hand, all new.

56

I finished my MFA and took a job teaching in Augusta, Georgia—the farthest-from-Michigan job I was offered. But family never quite leaves you, even, or maybe especially, *especially* if you leave them.

My sister called me one night in January of 2009. "Are you sitting down?" I knew what it was right away.

"Just tell me," I said. I did go and sit down, on the edge of the bed, to listen to her tell me that Dad had been arrested for bank robbery again. All I could think about was her. All of that difficult forgiveness, for nothing. Her anger utterly transformed her.

At that moment, listening to my sister unfold this new story of pain, her voice hard and burning with pure hurt, I remembered the way she looked as a fifteen-year-old the first time she went through this: sitting, so small in the overstuffed chair at Grandma's house, silent, burning in the dark, chewing her nails. Listening to her, I could have killed him that night. I could have shot him dead. I could have stared straight into his eyes and stabbed him in the gut.

I could have. A thousand miles from him all I had was my own skin to tear at. I didn't sleep that night, just sat up and stared and churned. In the morning I cleaned curls of skin and threads of dried blood out from under my fingernails.

It was one of the banks he had robbed before. He was described in the newspaper as wearing a trench coat, a tan fishing cap, dark glasses, a blue scarf, a black fanny pack, and Band-Aids on his fingertips. He waited in line. He walked up to the counter and pushed a slip toward the teller on which he had written in marker "I have a gun. All of your 10s, 20s, 50s, and 100s. No dye pack." He pulled a handgun out of his waistband and flashed it at her, saying, "No sudden moves." She placed $1,083 on the counter, including a pack of bait money. As he walked past the other people in line the dye pack burst early and red smoke seeped from the bag. He hurried out.

A man waiting outside, a heating-and-cooling technician on temporary disability with thyroid cancer, there to help his seventeen-year-old daughter set up a bank account for the first time, saw my dad rush by, cradling something "like a football," he said, but leaking red smoke, and knew it was a robbery. The man called to his daughter and her boyfriend to get back in the car fast and he chased my dad's old SUV, red smoke fluming from its window, the man on the phone with the police, updating them on his position. Nearby cop cars soon joined the pursuit. Dad pulled into a party store parking lot and lifted his hands off the steering wheel, raised them, and waited.

When the cops pulled up in a flurry of noise he refused to get out of the car. They dragged him out and forced him to the ground. The indictment states he was noncompliant. They Tasered him twice.

The local newspapers reported this story as "Hero Helps Police Nab Robber," etc, and the man received a commendation from the mayor and the police chief. "I was taught by my parents to always do the right thing," said the man at the press conference.

I have seen the photo of the man holding a plaque at this press conference, this good dad, a long dark scar across his neck where it had been slit open for his thyroid surgery, him and the police chief gesturing to a poster board with enlarged photos of my dad's gun, the note he used, his mug shot, the money spread out for display, and a dramatic close-up of my dad's red-stained hands zip-tied behind his back. Across the top of the poster board it says "Super Mario Bandit," flanked by two police shields.

"It was pretty cool," said the hero citizen about the final moments. "They had that big sawed-off shotgun pointed at his head. It was like watching a cop show live, right in front of us."

57

This gun, maybe the gun I saw under his bed as a kid. Maybe his girlfriend's. Anyway it wasn't loaded.

They charged him with three other local robberies but dropped two of them due to lack of evidence. It seems very likely he did these robberies too, but they couldn't prove it. He took a plea deal, and was sentenced to only ten years, well below the recommended twenty-five for armed robbery by a career criminal. He was ordered to pay $4,164 in restitution when he is released. He will be seventy-five years old.

And again, he dragged the proceedings out to two years, stalling on technicalities, this time so he could continue getting his pension and social security checks before he'd be sentenced. My sister was still trying to help him sort out his mess, still insisting on believing he loved her, or at least owed her, and he'd granted her power of attorney to manage his affairs and his money. But instead of paying my sister back what he'd stolen from her, he demanded that she use the last of his money to hire him a better lawyer. She said no.

"'It was so insane,' I told him. 'You don't need a better lawyer, Dad, it would just be a waste! They caught you literally *red handed*.' I begged him, I said, 'Please, for God's sake, just plead guilty, and be done with this,'" she told me. Then he wrote her one last letter, telling her he was turning his power of attorney over to his girlfriend and that she'd never hear from him again. He called her selfish and heartless, a bad daughter. And that was the last thing he said to her.

The psychiatrist who interviewed him during the trial was the same doctor who had assessed his mental health for the first trial, coincidentally. I read this report in the online court records. Dad describes his life as full of pain and anxiety. He suffered from incredible PTSD after his thirteen-month tour in Vietnam, where he served as a cannoneer/forward observer. He describes personally killing several Viet Cong. He was awarded a Bronze Star for bravery after leading a gun battle while on patrol with his platoon.

In the years after being honorably discharged from the Army, he describes the anxiety, depression, and addiction that led him into reckless speeding, cheating on his wives, drinking to oblivion, wasting money as fast as he could. He described mood swings that sounded a lot like bipolar depression to me, the same disease my mother has and one that I saw firsthand, daily. That especially killed me—him stealing her disease.

Eventually he describes hearing voices. "A military-type voice," egging him on to "Do it," rob a bank, taunting him during his severe depressive episodes. The psychiatrist does advise, with the dual-diagnosis of PTSD and gambling addiction, that Dad was in fact suffering from a "substantially reduced mental capacity at the time of committing the offenses." Not, as my dad hoped, though, certifiably insane. He was aware of his actions. He was described as "pleasant and polite" during the interviews.

This is Dad lying at his best. When I see how his manipulations work, really look at them, I see the truth. A great con starts with the truth. I think people can smell that, down there, under the elaborate scaffolding of lies, there is a truth, and this is why they're willing to buy the rest of it. More importantly, that mote of truth is what he himself must cling to. Some of that pain from the war and the incessant hurt of addiction is very real. After all, he had to convince himself first. I know that process. And I have no doubt he comes to believe his lies once they are built. They are well-designed. They organize the world.

Dad was always organized. Controlled and organized, he knew well enough to seem like a mess for the psychiatrist. But really, he was neat. He was a machinist, good with tools, precise even with repetition.

After again firing several public defenders, each one advising that he take a plea, he finally broke down. He did take a plea. He wouldn't, though, admit guilt.

The truth of the act, the plain cold insanity of the act, would be harder to accept, and he knew that. He gave whoever would listen a clean explanation and of course they clung to it. He was old, he was sick with kidney disease, he was a war veteran, he had an untreated gambling addiction, untreated PTSD from Vietnam, and he had three letters of support for leniency in his sentencing: one from his girlfriend, one from his sister, and one from me. I read these letters when I opened the public records from this trial.

His sister's letter describes her honest astonishment. This is not the man she knows; this is not her little brother. To her, he is a good man who made bad choices, for the only reasons that can be blamed—the war, the trauma. She is a kind, generous, honest woman, praising his work ethic, his generosity and dedication to his daughters, to whom "he gave everything." Her support for my dad has been unwavering. She was the one who recounted for me her childhood in a Nazi concentration camp. In her I see a familial dedication that my dad espoused but usually failed to actualize. Because in the end, it was almost nothing but us—his family, and our normalcy—that he compromised in the pursuit of his goals.

The letter from his girlfriend describes his tortured struggles with PTSD and flashbacks to a degree unrecognizable to me. She is a sweet woman, obedient to him, incredibly so, even after his serious deceits had been revealed to her.

The letter describes him waking up sweating and screaming at night, things like "Oh no! Oh my God it's a kid!" and "Get down, get down, incoming! We have to get them out NOW!" Two or three nights a week, she said, but he never wanted to talk about it in the morning. She was a wealthy widow, and explains he had access to her accounts but never touched them. He slept in a chair for a month in her hospital room while she recovered from a heart attack. After his arrest, she came home to find the FBI had broken down her door and were searching her apartment for the money. This was how she found out about his criminal past. She's dedicated to him still, driving to Ohio every few months to visit him there.

Here is my letter. I don't know if he read it.

Honorable Judge Battani,

I hope you take this letter into consideration when you sentence my father, Joseph Brodak, in a few weeks. Certainly he is guilty of these crimes, but he does deserve some leniency in regards to his sentence. He is a peaceful man who I have never known to physically hurt anyone and I do hope you will not sentence him to reside among violent criminals. I am pleased he took a plea bargain instead of wasting tax-payers' money on a trial. I know this took some humility for him. Furthermore, he is an old man with kidney problems, and I believe he should be placed in a medical facility if possible. I expect I will never see him again, and would be happy to know he is being taken care of in his twilight years.

He was in holding in Detroit county jail after his arrest. A dirty, crowded jail, not far from where he grew up. My sister went to visit him. He refused to see her. Before she left she put a little money in his account, enough for toothpaste and extra socks and things they don't give you there. She would have nothing to do with him going forward, and has kept this resolve since that day.

58

I always dismissed Dad's claims of PTSD, assuming this was just another con, but I came back to them eventually. Maybe he did really have this, having actually been through Vietnam—I owed it to him to at least consider it.

So I asked Mom at Christmas. After everyone had left I sat with her on the couch in the dark living room and just blurted it out. "I know it wasn't your specialty as a therapist, but do you think my dad really did have PTSD? In your professional opinion? And personal one, too, I guess."

She knitted her brows seriously and squinted. I could see her immediate reaction was a giant, silent *no*. But, she liked being thorough and equitable, like me, so she considered it. She thought quietly for a moment.

"There's a lot about your dad no one knows."

It was a stunningly fair thing to say.

"But, I've known him a long time. And lived with him for years and years. And I never once saw evidence of PTSD. The panic attacks, the fear, depression—none of that. And while it isn't my specialty, I certainly would know it if I saw it."

It's described as a "disease of time" in David J. Morris's book *The Evil Hours*, a heart-wrenching investigation of the disorder by someone who suffers from it daily. Time loses its linear shape and the past becomes mashed with the present, spinning bits of horror into a normal day. Imagine: at your desk, at the checkout in the grocery store—war washes over you. And it's more than just a memory, as you or I would remember some hurt from the past and cringe or buckle—it's a whole experience come back. The body feels it. And the body doesn't know the difference between real and imagined— it feels it either way. The body *doesn't know* the difference. Heart rate soars, blood pressure and adrenaline spike, real fear courses through the body. Time loops unpredictably and uncontrollably.

And it's hard to hide.

"But," Mom added, looking hard at me now, "probably you'll never find out the truth. No one knows your father. And he won't say what is true."

I nodded slowly, looking down.

"There you have it."

There I had it. Nothing.

59

S crolling down through the PDF of documents in the sentencing memo from this trial, I have to stop when I get to his letter. It's handwritten. His handwriting is pointedly emotional for me. All caps, thin pencil point, letters leaning on a forward slant. The voice loud and hard in my head as I read it.

He starts the letter with a description of himself. How he sees himself, for the judge's sake anyway. A "model citizen," he says, who pays taxes, votes, buys homes, raises daughters, works, works. On paper it looks so true:

```
The combination of PTSD and a serious gambling
addiction caused my life to change. Moreover,
my deeply rooted moral/religious values were
particularly compromised whenever I was faced
```

with financial chaos that threatened the status
quo of my family life, which I value more than
anything in the world.

Then the first crime: an unintended result from the
"trauma" of a job loss, and then prison, during which, he
notes, he "received no treatment for [his] real problems."

Then the next one, and he is sorry, and deeply regrets it,
and wants nothing more than to return to his family, whom
he misses dearly. *His family life, which he values more than
anything in the world. More than anything in the world.*

60

"You writing this," Mom said to me on the phone recently, "do you really think it's wise?"

"Wise how?" I asked, a little annoyed.

"I mean, won't he be pissed at you for writing a book about him? He might retaliate or something, or at least make it look like you fabricated it all . . ."

"I'm just saying exactly what happened, Mom, and I don't think that's wrong. Besides it's not about him, it's about me. And besides . . . I think he's a little different now. I'm not sure . . . he'd try to hurt me, really. I don't know if he has the energy for all that anymore . . ."

"Huh. I didn't know you thought he was different." She seemed bothered that I said that. "I guess men do soften up with old age. Still, you know him. He'd be totally pissed. He'd *say* you were making it all up. He'll never talk to you again when he finds out."

"I know. That's fine. Obviously I've thought about that and I'm fine with it if that's what happens. It was hard for me to decide to do this . . . but I'm proud of myself . . . even though it's kind of a . . . *risk* . . ." I sounded hurt and defensive, I knew. I wanted to feel supported in doing this. And she did support me, but shame and fear run circuits in families that are hard to undo.

"I just don't want him to ruin your life somehow."

I laughed.

61

I assumed the danger had passed. The crimes were done, Dad's influence on us was gone—what was left? What is always left: the story.

And the story is the most dangerous thing there is. Because the way we talk about what happened *becomes* what happened. Writing it down, not living it, was the greatest risk I'd take—the *finality* of a finished text, so whole, hiding its scaffolding, its messes, ineffable silences. How could I say what was true? A dad who was not the villain, a daughter who was not the hero, a story not of satisfying redemption but of discarding stories. There'd be no way to say it just right, and that was the thing I'd have to say.

Prison affords families the opportunity to study their inmate. It freezes the inmate in a structured space, apart from variables, and ensures the power is always in the hands of the outsider. At this safe distance, I could pry the lid from Dad's past, something he'd never once discussed with me when he was free. And his origin point, St. Albertus, was just a forty-minute drive from the suburbs where my sister and Mom now lived.

I wanted to see it for myself so I could stand where he stood at the beginning of his life, as a refugee just landed in a city about to crash down around him. On a visit home in December in 2012, the year I started this book, I snuck away for the day and drove myself there. I took I-75 to the Warren exit, the same exit I took when I worked at the College for Creative Studies while taking classes at Wayne State. Instead of turning right on Warren, toward the Cass Corridor and the New Center area still hanging on around Woodward Avenue, I turned left and continued down to St. Albertus Street, past train tracks and old factories.

There are a lot of death holes in Detroit. Not poor neighborhoods—beyond that. I mean nothingnesses, forsaken places. Scattered plots, some whole blocks, sets of streets, in the middle of the city; just dead places. The place my dad grew up is dead.

This area, around Mack and Chene just east of the central corridor, is one of the emptiest in Detroit. It is not the most dangerous; there just aren't many people here at all. Only a few structures stand on each block, and rarely are those structures occupied. Sometimes you can't really tell. Most houses are in different states of decay, some just piles of charred wood and ash. These are not the most picturesque ruins. They're not the famous ones, the Packard Plant or the huge train depot or the ornate and decrepit Michigan Theater. They're not the pretty ones, the derelict castles of Brush Park, raped over the years for their architectural embellishments and fireplace mantels, the unused skyscrapers downtown with wild trees growing atop them and floors full of artifacts, not the ones out-of-town journalists and photographers come to document, vaguely lament, then leave. These were plain poor houses to start with.

St. Albertus sits next to homes like these amid empty grassland. Across the street is one occupied house, and a heavily gated, new-but-cheap apartment complex, where a convent and girls' orphanage used to be. Behind the church is the school, a three-story sturdy brick building with a stone façade, "ST ALBERTVS," carved across a neoclassical frieze above four faceted pilasters between the doors. The school is a ruin, like any other building here. Windows are broken or still boarded, man-high graffiti covers the dark brick exterior, and the yard is well overgrown, with dumped TVs and furniture in the grass. I looked at the building for a long time. This was where my family first lived in America. This was where my dad learned English. I watched a solidly fat black squirrel climb the brick effortlessly, pause to eat a small thing on the windowsill, then disappear inside.

It shut me out like a secret. I wanted in.

On the front steps I pulled shyly at the boards over the three doors, but they were still nailed tight. It would be easy enough to climb up into any of the glassless first-floor windows but I was alone and it seemed unwise. I took some photos with my phone and just looked for a while at the building. A rind of green copper wound weakly around the roof, the rest of it having been pulled off by scavengers. *It would be very unwise to go in*, I thought. *I am just a girl by myself.* There could be squatters here, especially now that it was winter. Other times I had explored abandoned structures as all kids do who grow up around ruins, but never alone in such a desolate place. Still, here I was. I had come this far. I looked up and down the street, worried to leave my car out of sight, but there was not a soul around. I walked quickly to an inner corner and hoisted myself up on the ledge, then into the same glassless window the black squirrel had disappeared into.

Broken glass and soft piles of crumbled plaster. Cold dark. The smell of old wet wood and dead animals. I dropped down into a classroom, mottled white and brown with gritty gray floors. But there was some maintenance here, by the church people; I could tell the floor had been swept occasionally. I walked as if I was stepping on someone. The boards shivered and the sound of a steady wind hushed me.

A dark wooden door led to the hall, lined with more classrooms. All of the doorknobs were stolen. The next room was sweet sky blue, paint peeling at the top, with a chalkboard but no furniture. There was a red fire alarm box. Very nice wood, rotting, carved oak and maybe walnut. Powdery plaster made the ground soft. Every surface peeling. The next room was pale acid green, with a patch of exposed cinderblocks where the chalkboard was. It's hard to imagine my father as a boy, although I suppose that is normal. He was a star athlete, he'd told me. Captain of the football team in high school. He would've been a fun boy. Quiet but brave and strong, like me. I kicked lightly at some planks on the ground and the sound of scurrying claws in the walls moved away from me.

I went slowly down the hall, feeling ridiculous for using the flashlight feature on my expensive phone but glad to have it, since the floorboards poked up and warped unevenly, with odd piles of glass, nails, and splinters. The bare rooms felt heavy and full. I came to a stairwell. Plaster dust had been swept into loose mounds against the wall, and footprints marked a center path up the steps. I wanted to see the up-stairs, the large auditorium where they lived; maybe there'd be more left up there, furniture or books, interesting things maybe. I didn't feel bad for trespassing. I deserved to be here, somehow, to be a person who wanted to see what was good here and come to know it. Being in an empty building in an empty city feels like a pit within a pit, airless, a tomb.

On the second floor I turned toward the front of the building, to see the entrance room. The windows were heav-ily boarded and it was dark. The front room was nothing but a wide staircase leading to the three boarded entrance doors I pulled at. Thin cracks of blue daylight under the doors. Strange half-columns flanked the stairs, but no railing. Blackness at the bottom of the stairs; it looked like a boat landing, like dark water down there. The ceiling was bare above. The sight of the stairs shook me. I saw my dad running up these steps.

I backed out and saw another staircase going up, to the large room above. Some corny graffiti here and there, some beer cans and food trash. Swatches of paint peeled away from cracks in the walls, snaking leafy fronds of paint chips to the ceiling. The hall opened into the auditorium. The windows were not boarded up here and the room was bright, open, and cold. I stood astounded. On one end, a gaping black stage was framed with pale peach and jaunty blue leaf patterns, deco style, and flanked by two doors topped with Greek urns and vines of plaster. Straight across the stage hung a very small, gold-fringed, pale blue curtain, painted with mounds of red and orange flowers with wispy grass behind.

My mouth hung dumbly and I started to cry. The peeling colors and the light of the room, the flowered curtain and the darkness, the piles of plaster powder, the good wood, the still air. It was beautiful in a way I recognized in the oldest part of me. I felt like I was seeing something true for once. Indisputable. I walked the thin boards of the floor to the center of the room, past a large blue "A" painted inside of a circle, like a tidied-up anarchy symbol. Bird shit covered the floor, concentrating under vents. The cooing and wheezing and claws of pigeons echoed blindly. Above the center of the room, on the high ceiling bowed up like a coffin top, was a trinity of large pale blue medallions, the center one probably once surrounding a light fixture that was now gone. Scallop-edged circles wound around it, along with a rim of curled endless wave shapes. The two outer medallions merged edges with the large center circle, both with hard-edged, spiny, weblike grates in their centers and finials on the outside edges. My family slept on cots in this room for months. They looked up at this. My dad as a child, scared and silent, packed in with the other refugees, looked up at this ceiling and thought about the future, this future I am in now. I was pinned to the spot by this useless beauty, grateful. It was there for them, this silent, mindless pattern; it had hung like love over the empty room.

I could hear two voices below. I went to the window and saw two men on bikes talking on the sidewalk; one went on while the other lingered slightly, near my car. I wanted to see more but I had to go back the way I came. The halls seemed darker now and the space shorter now that I knew it. Without thinking I returned to the window I'd come through and stopped, standing very still and staring. I guess I didn't want to leave. I liked it here. A flock of grackles outside squeaked like rusty scissors. I felt sorry for my dad. He was scared here, and angry. He felt the same as he grew and watched this place become empty and ruined.

I hopped up and out. The men near my car were gone. The yard was once covered in concrete but plants had eaten through it completely. Still, it was not natural; no emptiness is natural here. It is not empty. Hollows are full of bodiless feelings, networks of lives missing, invisible. Abandoned meanings. The feeling of a whole world having just been lifted up and away from the ground. What's here now is wild. But "urban prairie" sounds a lot nicer than it is—what's growing is tamped with trash. Chairs, televisions, couches, car parts, clothes, burned wood, ominous rusted barrels, some full of unknown liquid, drifts of food packaging, of paper and Styrofoam, and tires, lots of tires. Sick city trash. Rats, raccoons, wild dog packs, and yes, pheasants, as is reported; I have seen a few myself, but no foxes or deer, as some claim.

Many plants here are abandoned ornamentals, once purchased and planted by the property owners, now weird, out of place and overgrown, like the beds of feathery common reeds in the wetter areas that mass over native plants in huge swaths, or crazily hunchbacked Japanese maples that used to flank front steps or paths. I walked slow through bony chicory stems and dried-out Queen Anne's Lace, still tough to pick, even dry. Mostly tall plain grass, dead stiff and upright, clubs of a grass I didn't recognize, some dry purple loosestrife. Burrs. Weeds. A lot of plants people hate, left in peace here.

The sky can be solid gray in Michigan, like wet concrete, churning without breaking for days. Under it, my home, sinking into the earth, the earth digesting its own paradox, in silence.

62

I walked to the front of the block, to the church. Unlike the school building, it was surrounded by a heavy black gate that was locked in all places except for the very front. I walked through the gate. The church loomed tall up close. The green copper roof and red brick were bright in the ash sky of December. It is light Gothic revival style, built in 1885, the oldest Polish church in Detroit, with a clock on each side of the steeple, all stopped at nine o'clock. The stained glass windows had been fitted with plain exterior windows for protection, but some were bowed and warped or missing. Only the two flanking entrance doors still had their elaborately branched wrought-iron hinges; the main doors had only ghost images of where the iron had been. I approached the doors and pushed the cold black thumb latch down. The enormous door was soundless.

"Eh, hello," a man said uncomfortably as soon as the door opened. He was on a ladder, messing with wiring that led to a set of light switches. "Just looking around," I said, and smiled, and he turned back to his work with some annoyance. I walked through a set of open plain glass doors into the body of the church, above which hung the inscription *Dom mój jest domem modlitwy:* My house is a house of prayer.

The ribbed vaulted ceiling was vivid pale blue, painted with gold stars and small murals, in near-pristine condition. The carpet down the center aisle was bright red and thick. The colors of the paint and stained glass were primary, carnivalesque, full of intense detail: the heavy red and white of Poland's flag, the Polish eagle. Polish and Latin inscriptions anchored the windows and portals. The space had been well maintained by the Polish American Historic Site Association, whose name was made clear on donation boxes, pamphlets, and plaques.

A table covered in red cloth to the left was laid with framed photos of the church, or pictures of priests and popes. Before the pews were more tables, covered with bricks engraved with donors' names; nowhere for them to go yet, I guessed. Tapestry flags with saints' faces dotted the spaces below the stained glass windows. Gaudy patches of red and blue stripes surrounded the stained glass windows. I moved down the aisle, past rows of heavy, plain pews, to an old nativity scene that had been set up for Christmas. The painted plaster figures knelt on old Astroturf, huddled into a barn diorama laid with pine boughs and a spiky white star atop the roof. A dusty bank of candles faced a life-sized Mary wearing an enormous gold crown. Clutters of images and sculptures of saints, popes, angels, and crucifixes activated every space. The altar and the baroque detail of the apse were covered in gold. *Królowo Polski wstaw się za nami,* it said: Queen of Poland, remain with us.

I had to stop and sit on the edge of a pew. The dense ornamentation of the space, how it hovered over my small body, felt cruel with its richness. This was my family's singular haven: their beacon of love and protection after years of horror. But I felt guilty for being here. Unlike at the abandoned school, rotting and dark, I felt unwelcome here, in my heart, a trespasser. I was not expecting this. But maybe a nonbeliever always feels like a fraud in church. I stood and turned back toward the entrance, the high polished marble columns shining, the enormous silver pipes of the organ way up on the balcony above the doors, the gleam and pull of the rich colors dense around me—an environment the opposite of the dark neglect of the school, its invisible fullness. There was fear here too, but made solid and showy. I didn't feel surrounded here, but drained in a way I didn't expect. I had to go.

63

A few weeks after the visit I wrote Dad to tell him that I saw the church, but I didn't tell him I went in. A letter came about a week later that opened with "You got to see St. Albertus Church!" The rest of the four-page letter described it to me, and the neighborhood, in more detail. He seemed surprised I was interested. His letters never say enough for me, never feel thoroughly human, just factual, but this one was at least excited in tone.

The first detail he tells me about is the black wrought-iron fence around the church. "One year I helped paint that fence and I grew tired of the paintbrush. I dipped my hands into the paint cans and applied the black stuff like that, because it was faster." Insane, I thought. I wondered if he was lying. It didn't matter. I loved this detail, even as a lie, for showing his devotion to St. Albertus.

He told me about his first job, selling early editions of the *Sunday Detroit Free Press* and the *Detroit News* after mass. He recounted the red wagon he used to haul the papers, the twenty-cent price of them, and the amount of money he'd make per day. He remembered specific details about his job, the wagon, and the neighborhood too, where the hardware store, the grocery store, the gas station, the specific shoe store, and clothing store on Chene were. He seemed proud, happy in his recollections, and he described work as if he loved it. He sounded not at all like a criminal.

I can't imagine being able to remember details like this about my own childhood neighborhoods, even though I am much younger. But certainly the neighborhoods were bigger, and there were more of them. All in all I moved six times before high school, changing schools each year of elementary school. Probably I am different, too. I don't like remembering these places: the friendlessness, isolation, and shame.

At the end of the letter I felt a pang. He wrote, "Thanks for the email. You got me thinking about the old school and church. Someday I'll drive you down there and show you all the places that were part of my past."

I couldn't place this emotion. It was sweet, of course, that he wanted to do this with me, nice to think of him showing me his neighborhood, how happy he'd be to do that. How alien it would be to him now, though. The sadness of the idea pained me. And to realize that he will get out of prison again. Not too long, really, just a few years left now, if he showed good behavior. This is his life. I pictured me driving him to Old

Poletown, him pointing out the window to the empty spaces and describing what was there.

I felt a kind of rage, anger at my own stupid selfishness, but there it was: the feeling I had before, when he was getting out the last time. I wanted him to leave me for good. To just die or go away forever, stop coming back like this.

64

A giraffe is nuzzling against a second giraffe. It sees me in my bright running clothes and looks, and I feel like I've won a prize in its regarding me. It is about midway through my morning run in Grant Park, on the backside of Zoo Atlanta, where there is a person-sized tear in the black fabric laid over the chain-link fence behind the giraffe/ostrich/warthog enclosure. Sometimes the giraffes cannot be seen, just a dull ostrich. Sometimes there is a khaki zookeeper rinsing a concrete platform with a hose; sometimes there's nothing but the grassy manure smell. Today I am lucky. I'm lucky every day, even if it is just the manure smell. I live in a house very near to these giraffes.

The houses I have lived in felt more like boats than houses.

That a house is stable and rooted firmly in the earth is not just one fact of its matter—it's the *key* fact of its matter.

Or so it goes. Homes operate as shelter and bastion, ward and moral statement. But they are always headed somewhere, it seems to me. The precariousness of the stretches of normalcy in my life left me with the feeling of movement: I was always headed away from wherever I was.

I suppose I'm talking about entropy. Entropy, even to me, a cold realist, seems sad. But it shouldn't be—after all, it is the way of everything to fall apart. *It* is the key fact; it's just the slowness and smallness of our timescale that obscures entropy's chewing.

Bodies are temporary, homes are temporary. They resist gravity as long as they can.

I thought about these things while house shopping with my boyfriend in Atlanta. We'd been living in separate apartments for three years and that was enough. I liked the very first one we saw: it was at the end of a dead-end street, had beat-up wood floors and a calm yellowy light. It was perfect.

But we were dragged off to the next one and I loved it. The *second* one was perfect. The third one! This is how it went, for months. It was too easy for me to fit myself into anything we saw. Maybe even especially the dingy ones, and most of them in our price range were dingy.

Yes, the dingy ones especially, because I don't like nice places.

Growing up around Detroit some people get this kind of fierce defensiveness toward ruins. I know it looks from the outside pretty ridiculous—who in their right mind wouldn't want the ruins torn down and replaced with nice condos and yuppie markets?

It's hard to explain. It's not as if I *like* damage exactly, it's more that damaged things seem truer. The good maintenance of a new or cared-for thing or building is an artifice I want to see past. This isn't about death. Death is pretty clean, a clicking shut; it's life rot belongs to, it's survivors who see and smell the decay—this is living. It's a radical thing to accept.

Finally, anyway, we did land in an unkempt but up-and-coming corner of East Atlanta, in a brick ranch built in 1930 with a chicken coop and three chickens in the huge backyard, tire swing in the pecan tree. The real thing. Nicer than any house I've ever lived in.

Atlanta has just enough rot in this part of town to make me feel comfortable, but still, you know, has working street-lights and regular trash pickup. Almost every day I get to run around Grant Park and stop to see the giraffes through the hole in the fence, which is too nice for me, but I'm working on it.

Atlanta, risen from the ashes like a phoenix, exactly what my city couldn't do, and what I can do too if I just let ashes be ashes. Honest job, boyfriend, house, friends, all real and true: I have it all. Out of nothing.

65

The sky, solid and gray and quiet, how it stays in the North. Pulling up to the prison's entrance I had a feeling that I had seen this particular slope in a dream, this sign, these colors. The complex sat atop a treeless hill, one small intake building with enormous mirror-polished doors and the other buildings set farther back, in neat lawns, sidewalks, and activity fields. We walked up to the black mirror doors, watching ourselves approach, watching our watching silently.

My boyfriend and I got there at the beginning of visiting hours. Everyone else knew how to do this complicated process, for which there were no instructions, and were happy enough to explain them as I accidentally cut in line. Forms and ID were presented, a debit card for the vending machines inside, and everything else we brought was stored in a locker. Our names were called, hands stamped with something invisible, and we passed through a metal detector, joining a clump of visitors now on the far end of the building. We waited again, inspecting the photos on the wall of previous wardens and other prison officials, sort of joking about their names quietly, attentive and antsy. A man's arm poked through a small door and we presented our hands to a purple light it held that made the invisible stamp glow, then we lined up at the exit door.

Waiting at the exit, I stood next to a window that met the edge of the razor wire border and I could see that the razors were actually sharp on the wire, silly billows of it, clean and perfectly silver. As we neared the next building, there was a gate to the yard, where men in khaki were milling around on pathways. On the way out there were starlings perched in the razor wire, squeaking cheerily.

It was cold in the visiting room and we waited for him to come out. A tall square cinderblock room with bolted-down rows of molded chairs, a large blue wrestling mat for children to play on, an alcove of vending machines, and a raised station of guards—it was clean, noisy, full, and bright. I was nervous, at all points of this approach, but especially now. I felt myself resisting. When we left the hotel I did not want to drive to the prison. When we arrived at the prison I did not want to go in. When we were sitting waiting for him to come in I silently prayed that he would not come in.

But he did, and was shorter than I remember, with all white hair and deep wrinkles. I did not recognize him at first. I stood to approach him and he raised his palm to me and motioned to sit down while he went to the desk to check in

241

with the guards. He hugged me hard when he came over, and kissed my cheek. I could tell he was honestly happy to see us both.

Here I was, visiting my dad in prison again, just like I did when I was fifteen, now more than twice as old. What was I looking for? What was I really expecting from him?

Most of what we talked about during the visit was food. He was not allowed to go to the vending machines, so he had to tell us what he wanted and we would go purchase it from the machines with the prepaid debit card we bought. He wanted pizza, and then when he finished the pizza he wanted another pizza. I felt terrible that he'd be the only one eating, so I bought a chicken sandwich just to eat with him. It came in a paper tray and was just foamy chicken on bread that after microwaving in the bag was wet and sort of warm, but still frozen in the middle. I ate half, and when I put it down he ate the rest of it. He asked for a Dr Pepper and Funyuns but they did not have Funyuns. I bought him jalapeño cheese curls instead, figuring those were the closest in texture to the Funyuns, but he did not much like them. While talking, he took a napkin to one curl and tried to wipe off the bright green particles that were making the curls spicy. On the next curl he seemed too embarrassed to use the napkin again, so he shyly scraped the curl against the edge of the bag to try to remove the flavor dust. I sort of watched him do that, and hoped it worked, though it probably didn't. He talked about the kind of foods he eats for dinner, and what was available in the commissary store. He said he buys ice cream once a week and sometimes tortilla wraps and tuna, which he fixes himself if he doesn't like the dinner offered. The bandit chewed his snacks. He spoke calmly.

The parts of prison life he seemed most pleased with were the activities and freedoms he enjoyed in minimum, boasting how there were two softball fields here instead of just one at the last place. At times he seemed downright happy about prison life, and it really didn't seem like an act. It's sort of easy there, with its stability, isolation from real-world problems, and petty freedoms—most of all the petty freedoms. His choices are limited, obviously—this seems to be in fact the philosophy behind incarceration—but not so limited that he feels he has no choices. He can apply for different jobs (his current job was rolling silverware into a napkin from ten in the morning until one in the afternoon, Monday through Friday, for which he is paid twelve cents an hour), play softball, basketball, or bocce ball, email or write to family, talk on the phone, read, or sit by the bocce ball courts and eat ice cream.

He explained how there were three different TV rooms— "one for whites, one for blacks, and one for Mexicans." It was not segregation, he insisted, just practical—it prevented arguments over which station to watch. In the room with mostly whites he watched the Discovery Channel, AMC, baseball when it was on, and football of course. The false dream of peaceful segregation that never worked in Detroit came to life in prison.

He was taking a World Geography class on Saturdays, although he told me he would have preferred the Home Wiring or Real Estate classes, but they were full. He can apply for other prisons if he wants. In fact he is applying to be moved to Milan, Michigan—where he had been incarcerated before—because they have some "religious program" there he described that if he can complete will knock a year off of his sentence. "There's also a drug one," he said, "but I don't qualify for that." It didn't matter; it seemed to be just a way to cut a corner.

He seemed like a gentle old man. He talked about his brothers and sister, and asked me about family members who don't want to talk to him anymore, like my sister. I tried to stay vague, as she would want. She'd told me never to talk about her to him, and I respected that. She didn't want him to know where she lived now, or where she worked. I saw a hardened hurt in his eyes, even during the soft talk, smiling, and casual jokes, a steady hardness. There was a pointed anger. Maybe it was shame. Or maybe just cultivated for his surroundings. Maybe it was not there at all and I just was looking for it.

Visiting hours were until nine at night, and I could tell the other visitors were settling in for the entire stay—staking small seating areas, loading up on food and drinks, setting out toys and books with their children. Most of the young children seemed happy and excited, some running up to the inmate as soon as he appeared in the room, many spread out on foam mats with their dads, toys everywhere, pleasant and good. Older kids, though, seemed different. One chubby preteen Mexican boy was crying, arms folded across his chest protectively, while his inmate dad talked close to his face intensely. Some girlfriends or wives seemed unhappy. I probably seemed a little unhappy, or nervous, squeezing my hands together and hunching forward in my chair. I tried very hard, though, not to seem unhappy.

Dad sat with his arm wide across the chair next to him, leaning back, not unhappy. Tranquil with us, as if we were visiting him at his private summer home.

Dad had purchased three photos in anticipation of our visit. We walked over to an inmate sitting at a table with a nice Nikon camera and a clipboard. "One of you guys, one of me and Molly, and one of Molly by herself," he said, having clearly planned this out in advance. My boyfriend and I stood with our backs to a solid blue backdrop painted on the cinderblock wall. I smiled. Dad stood by the cameraman and smiled. He switched with my boyfriend and put his arm around me and I smiled. He left me and I stood against the wall alone, feeling the space around me, the weird look of the cameraman on me, and my boyfriend and Dad smiling at me, and I tried to smile best of all. The inmate turned the camera around to show me the pictures. They were heartbreaking. I looked scared and small and too old to be anybody's daughter. I smiled. "Cool, they look great," I said.

It had been almost two hours and I felt like there was nothing left to say. I hadn't broached any real or remotely important topic, despite how much I wanted to ask him about the robberies. I told him we should be getting back soon. He seemed robotic in his reaction to this, switching away from us quickly, without hesitation or longing for us to stay. I looked at him a little more steadily now that we were leaving. He looked blank.

He hugged us, patted our backs, and turned to go without looking back, the way in which I also tend to leave. I hate to look back because it makes me sad to see departure too closely, but his reason seemed different. The small upbeat man with the comically huge ring of keys who led us in now led us out. He showed us a deck of ID cards and sorted through them slowly so we could pick ourselves out. It seemed as if we were the first visitors to leave. Outside the sky was still gray and solid with clouds.

When I had visited my dad in prison as a fifteen-year-old he had seemed stronger and more confident. And that act was still in place, but below it I sensed a frailty that made me feel sorry for him. I thought about St. Albertus, ruined, and I felt sorry for him. Maybe it was just that I was older and couldn't be fooled so well, or maybe the frailty had been there all along but I didn't recognize it.

I had pictured myself crying afterward. I had thought about how happy I would be to have my boyfriend there, someone to finally see and understand this strangeness. But I didn't cry. We walked out of the prison into the dull evening and I felt neutral, a little lifted even, partly from feeling as if I had fulfilled a duty in visiting him, and also in just leaving that place and entering the total raggedness of the whole rest of the world.

66

The next day we were in Detroit, in a casino, walking the labyrinthine floors of slot machines with my sister and my best friend Lindsey. My boyfriend went upstairs to play poker while we wasted money on slots and drinks. I examined the people as I wove around through the crowds and insect noises of the machines. The air of the enormous room felt thick—steeped in smoke, alcohol, and fried food smells—and I had to remind myself these were games. They were exciting games adults chose to spend money on for fun. Almost everyone seemed miserable, locked in the narrow focus of his or her game.

I had not spent much time in casinos and had stayed away from gambling, purposefully, not wanting to know how to play poker or whatever card games my friends or family played. Here, in the casino, I registered my disgust with the seductiveness of the environment. Low warm lights, soft curving mazes of machines and table games, the drinks and the buffets, a feeling of envelopment in a non-world, neither night nor day, a floating zone outside regular concerns. Women seemed to populate the massive plots of machines spread around cramped curved tables where mostly men gambled on cards or roulette. Men stood tensely at craps tables, focused. Men and women sat at blackjack tables stolidly, more slumped there.

I wanted to see if I could feel gambling for the fun it was supposed to be. I wanted to know if I could enjoy risk like my dad did. I found a mostly empty five-dollar table with all women and sat down, put my money in front of the momish dealer, and told her I had never played blackjack before.

Of all the casino games, blackjack had to be Dad's. My sister had told me as much when I asked her what exactly he was losing money on at the casino. He wasn't patient enough for poker, not foolish enough for roulette or craps, not braindead enough for slots. Blackjack is fast, repetitive, and offers players an illusion of control, which would have appealed to Dad.

I knew the basic premise, but no strategy on exactly when it's best to hit or stand. Least of all, I didn't know what counting cards meant, not that I would be good or fast enough with math to focus on it anyway. The dealer seemed tired and distracted, but perfectly practiced at being friendly, a good comfort. Her hand motions were perfunctory, a little lazy, exaggerating the clarity of the actions, I assumed for the benefit of the cameras overhead. Three older women sat at the table with me. Once I told them this was my first time playing they wanted to help me too, gesturing the tap (hit) or wave-wipe (stand) hand motions to me, sometimes to suggest what to do with each hand, and made sympathetic "aww" noises when I lost. The women were sweet, in fresh perms and holiday sweatshirts, playing slowly, like me, and chatting, knitting us together, not against the dealer or each other but the cards themselves. One talked about a blackjack tournament she'd just left, how it was too different and too aggressive. "I prefer this. Just sitting here, no pressure," she said and laughed, and the other women laughed too.

Another woman sat down at the table, remarking that she was glad to find a table "with just us gals." She caught on that I was new and brought out a wallet-sized, color-coded chart of instructions on how to play every hand. "You can buy these, you know, and bring this to the table even to check it. It tells you just what to do." The oldest one elbowed me and said, "See, we all in it together. Nobody plays against nobody, that's why I like it." It was true. At the table, as shy and cold as I thought I would be there, and as resistant and ignorant as I was to what I was doing, I began to see it right.

It was clearer, lighter, and more social than I imagined it to be. Against a glut of noise and choices beyond the table, the restraint on my choices, my movements, the outcomes of them, and the fixed loop of play settled me out of myself, into a simpler consciousness. A trustworthy routine, one thing to do at a time: one card to watch, flip, and react to, nothing else.

In a few minutes I doubled my money. Then lost some, then tripled it. "Beginner's luck!" the women said. I began to feel the split between my sensible urge to walk away and the loopy push to keep going. Because however much you have won, there is always a new hand; there is always more money than what you have. And the ritual of the new deal looks just like the last deal: timelessness. I stayed, and lost a bit, back to having just doubled my money. I got up, felt good about leaving, and liked having the chips in my coat pocket. The money you win gambling is better than money. It is converted into meaning. It affirms you. You made the right choices, you are smart, you took risks and it made your life better. No work, just money. Out of nothing, and so fast.

The goal, I suppose you must call it that, is not particularly to win, but to keep playing. Gamblers and psychologists will both tell you this. Of course, a gambler always has a finite budget, so to keep playing one must win, but the distinction is important. A stretch of gambling is living a whole little life in one sitting, plugging into a faster unfolding of contingencies: wins and losses come logically, clearly, fairly dealt. The proportion of control and providence *seems* balanceable, with just a little more cleverness. A whole life. No wonder we want to keep playing.

67

After a drink at the bar, I went back to the blackjack table. The dealer now was a sour, quiet man who seemed less patient with my lack of experience and slowness with simple math. The night had brought a younger crowd, more excitable and loose. The smoke was thicker and whoops and group cheers pushed through the crowds. Shifty, quiet players came and went, unlike the old ladies. There were men in leather jackets and baseball caps, alone, drunk couples, often arguing, and middle-aged women more interested in flirting than the game. Right away I won again, and then kept playing. The dealer scoffed at me when I didn't know to split my aces. The other players were barely watching each other. I lost all my money. The money that transforms into play credits, meaning-chips, is the vehicle into this identity-less loop, and when it is gone, so is the loop. Down to my last five dollars, I thought seriously about going a few steps over to the ATM so I could take out more. But when I got up from the table and walked in the direction of the lobby, where I could feel the outdoor air buffeting in from the endlessly moving revolving door, and remembered the real world, I didn't want to go back.

I didn't like it. I didn't think it was evil, just shallow and wasteful. I don't enjoy risk, the "thrill" is just anxiety to me, and I couldn't exactly afford to gamble anyway. While my chips were being pulled away from me I tried to remember the feeling of the lost bills in my hand and calculate what food or gas they could buy, to punish myself with the thought. Nothing here was sexy, except the forgetting maybe, especially the forgetting of the odds. The neatness of complete escape: a hospital bed, a farm—a gambling table, I see now. The elaborate regularity of the ritual, the feeling of possibility paired with the insane secret confidence all players seemed to have: *they* will be the ones to outwit this unfair game, and it could be *this* next spin/card/roll that will make up for all the others that kept them there. Absorption. It reminded me of what Dad liked about church. It reminded me of where he was now.

Thousands of people in thousands of tiny, locked game-dreams, suspended in timeless cycles, pointed in the kind of focus that hope or pain induces. Fun. But sick. I never felt comfortable enough with escapist self-indulgence, or even regular comfort most of the time; absorption sickened me—couldn't *let* myself go too far. I sometimes think it is because I was afraid of letting myself be happy, because I hated that self somewhat, didn't think I deserved it.

Also I tend to think it's healthier to enter the pain of the world and see its insides than to block it. I suppose this is me writing this now. I don't actually know if it is healthier.

Foucault describes the environment of prisons as "an architecture that would operate to transform individuals: to act on those it shelters, to provide a hold on their conduct." The prison we'd just visited imprinted upon us with authority the seriousness of its message: this is a place of punishment. We listened—we were quiet, kept our heads down, moved obediently, with respect. The next day in the casino acted upon us as its counterpoint: it encouraged a similar loss of self and time, but voluntary. Both replaced the mess of the world with a tidier one.

In these pseudo worlds my dad gave himself over. They controlled him away from us, away from the ordinariness of work and boring family life and debts. I don't think he would admit he ever wanted to surrender himself to the casino. Or to prison. He might say he felt helpless against them. In the lobby of the casino I sat on a bench and watched gamblers shuffling into the dark gaming cavern. I searched their faces. Were they helpless? Were they fine, happy even? In sweatpants, in leather jackets, in cowboy hats, in puffy coats, in a daze or laughing or with fierce energy, they came in for a bit of fun. I imagined my dad being compelled into the dark room, steely eyed and drained, aiming only to make enough back for the mortgage or to stop a bookie's threats, a victim of too much fun. I reimagined him as no victim at all but a perpetrator, a callous cheat, his chest lifted, shoulders straight, smiling calmly. On a winning day I imagine he walked out as the latter. On a losing day, well, there was always tomorrow.

68

Money is already a metaphor for something else. It is not so much a thing but an agreement among people, a relation, and has no real immediacy in its solid form—the coins and paper and plastic cards don't *do* anything, don't function as objects, but as concepts, promises. In a regular exchange, it stands in for a person's time, or some materials, food, honest work. In gambling the metaphor is doubled and in its doubling its relation is smeared: those things converted into money, then money converted into credits, distances you from time, materials, honesty. But the conversion of cash into gambling chips is not a conversion, not really; it's a purchase, a done deal. You buy a little chance to prove yourself. You buy a little time to do something simple. The credits or chips hold a ghost of a ghost. The money is already gone.

Maybe gambling abstracted money too much for him, prepared him, psychologically, to commit crimes for it. "Money forces humans to reduce qualitative differences to quantitative ones. It forces a numbering of things," writes Jack Weatherford in *The History of Money*. The hope for numbering impossible intangibles must bore even harder into a gambler's relations with money. If Dad was in serious trouble with bookies, or dangerously overdue on bills, he had family he could've turned to. How his list of sensible options was turned upside down so that robbing banks was on top and asking family for help was on the bottom has everything to do with feelings. Unquantifiable, uncountable, uncontrollable feelings—fear, mostly.

I can't say for sure how he felt about money. But I myself know what it's like to steal. It felt just like gaining credits to continue, symbols I neither deserved nor honored beyond their immediate exchange for some of the things that ran my life. To continue is what mattered most.

Now money operates for me as a dull and unpleasant necessity, as it does for other creative people who don't directly pursue it in itself. If I have enough, I don't care beyond that, and I have certainly not been particularly good at keeping it, although I am getting much better.

No, I hate money. I resent its power. Meaningless, bodiless, total power. And I resented the people who bought those stolen goods from me online years ago, knowing their money was likely honest, and their honesty was touching my dishonesty in the exchange, exposing it more brightly to me and just to me. I used their honesty, and I envied it.

Dad did the same thing with our trust. He *cheated*. In Caillois's *The Definition of Play*, he describes cheating in games as simply another way to *use* the rules, paradoxically, to keep playing, like any other player wants: "If a cheat violates the rules, he at least pretends to respect them. He takes advantage of the other players' loyalty to the rules."

My sister walks into a bank and uses her key to open the EMPLOYEES ONLY door, puts her nametag on, sits behind her window, and flips the CLOSED sign to OPEN. Her first job out of high school was at a bank, and she's never left. She accesses the bank in the exact opposite way of her father: honestly.

Years of working as an auto loan officer has left her conflicted. She likes being tasked with making the right decision—who should get what loan when, who has what credit and can handle what repayment schedule. But she sees it as unfair, heartbreaking. The amount of people with bad credit scores and enormous debt in a city like Detroit, under long-term economic depression, is staggering. Most people just want an auto loan so they can get a car to drive to work, since public transit is sorely lacking in the area. Every day she turns people down. The dealerships and the banks make their profits off an undereducated public when it comes to loans, and to her, it is a moral issue. I asked her once what kind of financial job she'd love and she said internal auditor, because "you just go in and tell people what they're doing wrong." I had to laugh a little. It was sweet, her unabashed directness. And she'd be good at that. She wants to set things right. It's rare, although it shouldn't be, that a person can thoroughly apply nothing but integrity to money.

I think it is a point of security for her, to work in a bank. It's a connection to him she probably would not consciously entertain. Also, I think she genuinely likes money. She is brilliant with it, saves and spends without error, has an inhumanly perfect credit score after years of rebuilding it from the damage Dad did to it, owns an enormous house on a golf course full of possessions she earned. She knows about money. I don't think it is a matter of respect. I think it is a matter of control.

69

Time, most importantly, is what money means. The money you bring into the casino is made out of your time. Meaning, made out of your living, your very life. And you use your lived-time to buy future-time to gamble. It's almost a kind of time-laundering.

Once settled in Detroit after Vietnam, Dad worked as a tool-and-die maker for GM, fabricating small metal parts all day. In the late eighties, though, all of that was automated or outsourced, so he was moved to the testing facility, where he took parts off of cars for engineers to test. He'd take them off, put them back on sometimes, or sometimes the whole rest of the car would be scrapped. He'd steal weird objects from work, coming home with enormous boxes of tiny paintbrushes, bolts, or obscure metal shapes that could not possibly have a purpose outside of the shop. In the garage he had drawers and boxes full of repeated, small objects.

In writing about Baudelaire, Walter Benjamin connects the distortion of time in gambling to the very same kind of work my dad did, factory work. He describes the similarity in terms of the compartmentalization of time:

> Gambling even contains the workman's gesture that is produced by the automatic operation, for there can be no game without the quick movement of the hand by which the stake is put down or a card is picked up. The manipulation of the worker at the machine has no connection with the preceding operation for the very reason that it is its exact repetition. Since each operation at the machine is just as screened off from the preceding operation as a *coup* in a game of chance is from the one that preceded it, the drudgery of the laborer is, in its own way, a counterpart to the drudgery of the gambler. The work of both is equally devoid of substance.

He goes on to explain that it is "devoid of substance" because the action is a repetition, and repetition drains meaning, it never adds up, never builds something whole. After all, the machinist doesn't make a car. He just keeps making parts, the same parts over and over, feeding the factory indefinitely. It was when Dad stopped making parts that he started going to the casinos for blackjack. The timelessness of repetitive, incompletable action was transferred from work to play. There is no end point to blackjack. The bodies change but the game goes on, *through* them, then beyond them, no matter what.

In the casino, time is not measured on clocks but in money. There are no clocks anywhere. Time is parceled into the repeated action, the hand or button-push or card-flip, not minutes or hours but *this* hand and then the next hand and so on—the result of which produces more money or less money. More play or less play. More time or less time.

The gambler's buy-in amount becomes the beginning of time, a starting point he is always trying to move away from. "Time" is money being added or subtracted to this origin point, so it can move forward or back. A smart gambler will stop when he is "ahead" or "up"—as reasonably far away from the origin point as he can get. To lose money, though, is to go back to the start. To lose beyond his buy-in doesn't make the addicted gambler stop, but want to push even more wildly away, to go on tilt, as they say. It's almost as if, for him, there is no back. There *must* be only forward. On tilt, a gambler is usually several real hours in, their passing almost in secret, in the unchanging zone of the casino, and physical exhaustion clouds reason too; the chase starts over.

Good gamblers let gambling train them to manage their emotions. To be specific, they learn to suppress. Meaning, lying to oneself that things are OK, the bad emotion caused by loss is not there, the guilt, regret, and anger is not there, until the lie sticks, and the gambling can continue with a level head. It can't be faked.

I don't know for sure if he had this self-control. But I do know he couldn't have been very good at gambling, after all. Being good at gambling requires this self-control, as well as skill and good money management.

Gamblers seek control at the same time they hope to escape it. It feels good to surrender to the trustworthy outcomes of gambling, to give over completely to the simple rhythm and singular focus of its movements. But the strong desire to control the game, to win it with skill, is in the forward mind, and keeps the addict chasing wins against all reason. And Dad played blackjack, a game the house wins, in the end. He bet on sports with big bookies, odds solidly against him. He lost and lost, persisted at losing.

To attempt to cope with absolute losses by *playing* at loss, repeating it, in safer scenarios that are of one's own choosing, is an old story. I considered this motive there, in the casino, surrounded by losers persisting at losing. Maybe gambling is a kind of wound-replay, wound-fascination, because it's so *obviously unwise* that it seems like self-harm.

I started thinking about Dad's wounds while we finished our meal in the casino. We sat in a booth overlooking the pit as if at the center of some Technicolor panopticon, the bells and squawks of the slots meshed into one grinding blare. Dad didn't know his dad; he was only told about him. This loss hung on him like a millstone. He saw his family structure dissolve as Detroit dissolved and St. Albertus dissolved. He came from war and went to war. He knew many losses. It has to be a kind of self-abuse, for certain, to replay losses, what

Freud called "repetition compulsion," but it *feels* empowering, because for once the loss is now one's choice. He would've said he was going to the casino to make money. Really he was throwing it away. Throwing away his money, meaning his time, meaning his self.

It's a way of being a little dead. It's a nice feeling, refreshing. Living is hard to do.

While I was wasting away in bed after my surgery I knew that feeling of being a little dead. I understand why sometimes people want to get sick. There are no particulars of self. But here, a choice to self-liquefy actively, persistently, is something more than what I experienced. Most addictions are cowardly, slow, burdensome suicide attempts.

Maybe the death-drive concept was all a bit much, though, I thought as I looked out onto the casino floor. Most people who gamble don't become addicted, don't resort to robbing banks to catch up with their debts. Lots of people didn't know their dads, lots of people return from war without ending up in jail. It's just a game, after all, something to draw the things in him out, to play with. Did there have to be something in him, under all of this, essentially primary, to blame?

70

Caught as he was, both times, what was it, exactly, that he had to say for himself? I wanted to read the transcript from the trials. The more recent trial materials were online, but the older ones were too old, I discovered. Frustrated, I finally went to the law library at the university where I teach; I couldn't get any further on the Internet. I waited patiently for the reference librarian to come back to her desk, upon which she had left an open bottle of apple juice and a printed-out email with the subject line "Re: Food at the Beach." She came back, a rich-looking, bird-y blond girl, and explained to me that the database I was using was the only one, really, and we looked at it together to see if we could get more out of it.

I watched her type my dad's name into a search field. I could tell she didn't type much, pecking with one thin finger, misspelling "Joseph" three times. Eventually she made a call and the person on the other line explained that any trial documents from that year, 1994, were just too old to be in the database, and that all I could do was go to the actual courthouse where he was tried and get photocopies from their files, which would be in storage, meaning their retrieval would be time-consuming and costly. The librarian kept asking me about the man I was researching. "What did he do?"

"He robbed banks."

"Why?" She had a coastal southern accent and unblinking eyes. I shrugged. "Are you sure you have his name right?"

"Yes."

"Exactly right? You sure there's not a 'c' in 'Brodak'? Sounds like maybe there could be a 'c' there . . ."

"Quite certain . . . it is my last name too."

"Oh, oh my, are you related? A distant relative?" she said, utterly joking, and exaggerated a smile, eyes blinking weirdly.

"It's my dad," I said through a pained smile.

Her mouth opened wide and she became a bit louder, which bothered me as the nearby circulation clerks could hear her increasingly astonished questions about my research. She wanted to know who I was and what I do and why I wanted to write this and what does everyone think of it. I answered her questions politely, but always with attempts to end the conversation. She was so loud now. "Well, that is amazing, I mean you might hear about a bank robber and think of what kind of person he is, but look at you, and you had one for a *dad*!" She laughed, and I am certain I laughed, but not for the reason she must've thought.

71

I took a break from my research to sit on a bench outside of the library, just watching a squirrel do its squirrel work and trying to stay open to the sunshine and leaf sound. The squirrel stopped in a patch of lawn to bury something, arching its back with all of its small power to dig a pretty pathetically shallow spot. It dropped the morsel in, then patted the grass down in that adorable but neurotic squirrel way. I thought about Dad shooting this squirrel.

No one would care. Squirrels are solitary mammals, meaning they live alone their entire adult lives, except for brief periods of mating or rearing babies. No other squirrel would miss this squirrel. Its little dark life—eating food, sleeping, and burying bits, all alone—seems to light up the network I'm sunk in. It looked at me with its inscrutable eye: *Why do you need so much more?*

Our species is social—intrinsically, irritatingly, helplessly social. It's enough to prove this with any emotional test: it's not even so much the people we insist on yoking ourselves to, but the *connections* themselves. We are attachers. We die without attachments. We spend most of our free time refining or maintaining our attachments. *Insisting* on them, even at great cost. Kids without families hurtle themselves at cobbled-together pseudo families—some loving friends, some insane gangs, some virtual worlds, some sad self-destroyers, cults and churches, too. Sometimes not people at all but things, feelings for things or actions, colors, movements, bells, and dings. It almost doesn't matter what, as long as there is a binding. As long as the soul is caught in some kind of net.

It seems logical to think that the natural order of life is to attach oneself to one's family, who in optimal conditions is automatically *there* and *good*, until the time comes to leave this supplied family and construct a new one to cleave to. And so it'd be logical to consider any disordered attachment—to objects, to drugs, to gambling—as an awful interference, an addiction: a disease! And to cure it would be to release the addict from his prison of unnatural attachment, and sail him back to his more wholesome network of friends and family.

Was Dad really an *addict*, exactly? If he was, did that mean he could be *cured* and sail back to us whole?

72

"Come in, come in!" a voice shouts when I knock. My boyfriend and sister and I walk out of the dark February cold into a warm home, lit all around with candles. It's Valentine's Day, and my sister has come to Atlanta to visit, and so we brought her along to our friends' dinner party.

Christiana in the kitchen with a dainty apron tied over her long party dress, hovering over the most enormous steaming pot of mashed potatoes I have ever seen. She's adding more cream and cream cheese and tasting it while Rusty, her husband, hesitates over the incredible tenderloin, knife in hand, not sure if it's ready to slice. Brian's wearing a nice suit and his girlfriend Tina hands me a beautiful coupe glass filled with a red drink. "Artillery Punch," she says, "it'll knock the chill off." I introduce my sister around and we sink into the couch by the bowls of pale roses and trailing ferns where Caroline, Christiana's sister, is regaling the group with a hilarious story of a coworker's breakdown. She might have had a tiara on. Even if she wasn't *exactly* wearing a tiara, she always seems as if she is wearing one, either of gems or flowers.

She's made party favors for everyone: framed photographs of each couple in attendance she printed off of our Facebook pages. "A photo of you and your person," she said when we saw them on the coffee table, "and you have two people!" One photo of me and my boyfriend, another of me and my sister when we were little—Christmastime, us in our dresses, eyes glittery upon the presents. My sister hugs Caroline, beaming.

We find our seats at a long table where Christiana has painted tiny name place cards for each one of us, even my sister, who is new. Each one decorated with a different flower, each name inked perfectly in Caroline's lovely cursive. We squeeze close to the table, which is stuffed with mismatched plates and set with dishes of fresh radishes, blackberries and mint, caviar and cheese crisps, the roast, the mountainous bowl of potatoes, the little cups of perfect crab bisque. Various stray fern fronds trailing out from the rose bouquets occasionally alight from some dripping candle, but someone always pinches it out in time. A toast to love is raised.

I hold my boyfriend's hand under the table and look around at all of it. Everyone is beautiful. And happy, happy in this closeness. Christiana, ever attentive to changing moods, sees some misty look in my face and plucks two vintage millinery flowers from who knows where and places one behind my ear, and the other behind my sister's. We hug and smile; someone takes a picture for Instagram.

My boyfriend and Rusty, friends since the second grade, start bickering as they always do about some dumb football thing, Christiana shouts to me across the table that she is in despair that we weren't seated next to each other, Brian and Tina are kissing, Tom is controlling the music with his phone, Christy is commenting on it, James and Carolina are dancing in their chairs, oblivious, and all of us are eating and smiling. I look at my sister. She looks at me and tilts her head and we are thinking the same thing. I am embarrassed by my happiness.

Dinner ends with the raspberry pavlova, lemon heart tarts, cherry vanilla fudge, and of course the cream puffs I made. People are stuffed, leaning in their chairs, dying of food joy. In the living room, someone cues up Fetty Wap and we have to leave just as everyone is drunk enough to start dancing. Out in the cold, on the way to the car, we huddle close, the glow of the party trailing from us like a comet.

The next day I take my sister to all the Atlanta attractions: the Coke museum, the zoo, the big Ferris wheel. At the end of the ride, photos of us are presented, at which of course I balk but my sister considers. They Photoshopped in the giant Ferris wheel behind us and added a sunny blue sky. My sister insists on buying the photos, even though it costs twenty-five dollars. She buys the accompanying plastic frame, too, when the cashier suggests it.

At home, the photo of us is added to the dinner party photos on the table. Outside, we sit on the porch swing, and I tell her about the book I'm writing.

"He's never going to talk to you again when he finds out."

"Oh yeah, I know. I give zero fucks."

"I mean. You just better mean that."

I know what she means. I don't give zero fucks and she knows it. But I made my choice.

"Us growing up . . . what did . . . I mean, how did you *show* me?" she asks, tenderly. It makes me crumple a little, pausing.

"I just told the truth. You were a stressed-out child, under a lot of pressure, and it showed. It wasn't easy for you and so I just described it. I know we didn't really get along when we were little, but it wasn't our fault really. Don't worry." I'm softening it up a bit, I know.

"I just want to make sure, even though I was bad at times, that it seems like I loved you."

I'm quiet for a minute and I look at her like *of course*. "I was so jealous of you," she added softly.

"Jealous of *me*? I was jealous of you!"

"You got to go with Mom. Mom loved you. She's a nut-case but at least she really loved you. Living with Dad sucked."

"I know."

We swung quietly on the swing for a bit. I thought about how much she used to hate me.

"I'm sorry, Boo. I wish you had never gone with him."

"Well, whatever. I guess I'm glad it was me and not you."

I was surprised at this. "Why?"

"I dunno. I was tough. I am tough. I handled it, then I got over it. And, I'm great now that he's gone. I have everything I want and he can't touch me." I smile at her.

"You are tough. I'm tough too. We're stupid tough."

"He's just a weak person. Somehow I'm glad. He showed me exactly how I wanted to not be."

73

It's the day after Thanksgiving and I forgot to write to him. I log into CorrLinks and check my inbox. No new messages from him in the past month. I try to find the last email exchange we had but it's all empty: the messages are only archived for thirty days, then they disappear.

I write to him as I'd write to a penpal—distanced, a little uncertain, with a plain dullness I know is shaped by the self-conscious awareness that someone screens these messages before he reads them, even though their content is never more than polite and bloodlessly broad life updates.

"How's the new job? Is it interesting?" I ask. I remember he told me he upgraded from a job rolling silverware in the kitchen to a "computer job" for two dollars a day—previewing patent applications and rejecting them if incomplete. "I got a new cat. She's kind of shy but funny, with one white spot right on her chest. Her name's Jupiter." I feel like I'm talking to a child. "Hope you are staying warm there!"

I eat lunch, grade papers, go for a walk, check back for a response, spurred by nagging and totally pointless guilt. No response. Over seventy now, with failing kidneys; I sometimes wonder if he'll make it to his release date. Or even to another email.

The day passes. I try to forget about him. Then, I do forget about him. Days slip by, weeks, and I just forget all about him, as I always do.

Almost a month later I receive a Christmas card from his girlfriend.

"Merry Christmas Molly—you're a doll!" it says. Below her signature is his, pressed on by a stamp she had made. Enclosed is a check for three hundred dollars, also with his "signature" stamped on it.

74

Addictions separate people from each other. The ones forsaken by their loved ones' addictions are abandoned, without access. If it is a disease, then it is treatable. If it is merely a choice, then it is a moral problem, and the behavior ought to be met with punishment, imprisonment, or worse—traditional corrective actions. I know the enlightened, scientific view of addiction as a disease has softened the stigma of addiction from moral depravity into almost a mental disability. And perhaps it is for some. This doesn't match up right with Dad.

The logic of addiction as a disease looks like this: faced with choices, people choose options or behaviors that are in their best interests. Since addictions are self-destructive, choosing that behavior, especially over and over, must be involuntary. If it is involuntary and destructive, it is a disease. The addict can't *learn* to get better, or be punished into recovery; he is a victim.

But people voluntarily choosing self-destructive behavior is ordinary. It is so ordinary to me, so regular, that it seems extraordinary to observe any consistently self-advancing actions in anyone for very long, let alone a lifetime. Perhaps that says something about my life. It shouldn't be rare to find a person taking absolutely good care of him or herself every single day. I think of myself as a good steward of my own self: my brain, my heart, and my body. But not always. Not every day. Not even every year. I choose awful things and actions. Repeatedly, even.

And small actions touch off other particular actions and events. The little blunders, dumb moves, accidents, the delays and distractions: a turn, a click. Lives build like so.

A poor choice is easier to make when the timescale is small and immediate. If I think of eating a small candy bar today against the range of other things I have eaten today, it doesn't seem so bad, fine even, against the salads and good snacks. But if I think of all the candy I have eaten all week, I think again. Gambling is the same. It is easy to not zoom out and see all the money at once, all the loss together. There's only *this hand*. There's only *tonight*. The little loss is OK. It's manageable. Recoverable maybe. The global loss is forgotten, and when considered, a hard perspective to maintain against the losses to be recovered and the pressing mood of the day and the ache of the now-you, which feels like the only you when you want something. A whole life of gambling would never be chosen as optimal, or even fun or good. But a night of gambling is often just that.

Did he not learn? He mostly lost at gambling. He mostly chose wrong. Over and over. Why can't I see him, then, as a helpless addict? I honestly ask myself. I think sometimes I just didn't know him enough, not like my sister or my mom did. But I think that's just fear. I did know him, as well as anyone did. My version of him is as true as every version he gave anyone. There are only versions.

I see this as meaning that he had a stable internal locus of control. Those with an external locus of control blame circumstances for their troubles, pray to God for change, await good luck, sink into victimhood at bad breaks, passively react to their lives instead of acting them out. The internal locus types believe in their own control, sometimes to the point of delusion, but generally don't blame others for their faults or successes, tend to not believe in fate, and force the world they want into existence, for better or worse. Most probably fall somewhere between the two extremes.

It seems as if criminals, once confronted with their crimes, almost universally blame external factors for their behavior, and my dad did just that in both his first and second trials. It was the war, it was PTSD, it was addiction, and anxiety from childhood. The causes were always so remote. The more remote, the less he could be expected to have control over them. It is a strategy for absolution of responsibility.

Of course, criminals do often have sad stories of abuse or trauma that certainly imprint themselves on their psyches for all time, like many noncriminals do too, but what seems to be a strong tendency to identify external loci of control is a hoax. It seems as if it is just the thing to say when one is caught. A criminal like my dad, a liar, has the most certain internal locus of control out of anyone; it is upon this that he relied unconditionally. A liar convinces himself first. That's the hardest part. But if it works, then convincing others becomes easy. Manipulation is opportunism in its fullest realization: it is directing that erases itself, even to the director. An opportunist is not waiting for conditions to align for the crime to work, he is making the crime work in conditions as they are. The circumstances of *self* change to fit. That is power.

I could never understand, even after having played, how any reasonable person could consider gambling, especially blackjack, as a winnable game. It looked like a closed situation to me: the house has the edge. But some inlet must be discovered, or more like manufactured, when a person feels intense self-control, especially one who looks for risks. It is a way to pry open any action that seems closed. Perhaps especially the actions that seem most sensibly closed, like a table game at a casino, which for the average player is unwinnable in the long run. Or, a bank full of secured, private money. A marriage, a family. Fixed things, things closed to interlopers, things he uprooted for himself.

To project one's values onto the world itself, in order to function agreeably within it, is everyone's life work; it is the criminal who takes no responsibility for anything *but* this. It is what Sartre called "bad faith," unencumbering oneself of effective messes, the trash that falls away from the missiles of the will. My dad's crimes seem hopelessly reckless, especially in their repetition, so much so that I had decided when he robbed again, after seven years of living normally with his family, that he simply wanted to go back to jail. After all, it could not be a mistake; he could not have thought he would get away with it. It *looked* like a choice.

I see him making choices rather than mistakes probably because I have a similar internal locus of control. So does my sister. Generally it is empowering, certainly, but frustrating when error does happen, when self-discipline breaks down or unlucky events can't be changed.

I don't know. I don't know if he is a sociopath. I do know he cheated at everything. He lied to everyone, kept us all away, and resisted every regular structure of civilization: work, family, entertainment, economics, love. If he thought he truly could get away with all the cheating, and an entire life of lying—and he did get away with it at first—then yes, there is something persistently demented in his thinking. But if he did it all, knowing the consequences, who and what he'd lose, and went ahead anyway—that seems like something else, like actual evil. The picture is really all of it at once. It is irreducible. And that seems true, truer than I am even saying here.

On a recent visit to my sister's house I found myself in her basement, using the exercise equipment down there instead of going for a run just because it was so cold out, and I have lost my tolerance for cold since moving to the South. I wandered over to a corner of the room where I recognized

Dad's tools and stuff from the garage of their last house. After his arrest, my sister just let the house go into foreclosure since it was so behind on the mortgage. And she seemed happy to abandon it. I was sort of surprised to find his stuff there then. The good tools made sense to keep, I guess, but some of these other things seemed weirder. It was all the stuff he'd taken from work. I started opening boxes and drawers.

Trays of hundreds of "wood-handled 2" paintbrushes, wrapped stacks of paper cups, small boxes of gold-wire braids and silver-wire braids, cut tacks, screw eyes, hook eyes, drill bits, silver washers and nuts, packs of dust masks, plastic S hooks, bags of black zip ties, green, red, blue, and yellow wall anchors, black screws, bags of flat silver triangles, coils of nylon rope, coils of snakelike hose, a bucket of white cotton gloves, hundreds of incredibly tiny light bulbs, twist ties, razor blades, metal hollow-handled paintbrushes, a box of tape rolls, and a box of small plastic boxes. An enormous hoard of little things. Stolen things. She kept them. Perhaps they'd be useful, like he thought they might be.

75

Artifacts, maybe, I needed artifacts to hold in my hands. I tore through my small apartment, emptying desk drawers and pulling boxes and photo albums from their shelves. *I have things he gave me*, I thought, *surely I do.*

I found notebooks of poems, old planners, school papers, graded essays from college or even high school, printed with teachers' praise that I could not part with. I found photos, small toys, childhood drawings: things everyone has.

Nothing from him, nothing. I sat on the floor and thought. Fresh out of prison, he bought me a used car, but I no longer have that. For one childhood birthday he gave me a porcelain figure of a blond woman in a blue dress, skirt spread out into a wavy cone, one arm holding a bouquet of flowers finished with blue rhinestones. It came with a little folded card printed with a birthstone rhyme, the one for March:

Aquamarine means courage,
I'm brave as I can be,
and never let anyone say
I'm afraid of anything I see!

Her head had broken clean off once, and was glued back on. I don't have that anymore either.

I tried, but couldn't remember anything else. I don't have anything from him. I don't have any possessions of his, not even accidentally.

I only have the square photo of himself he'd inscribed and given to Mom . . .

```
Nora,
    My first real, true love. You changed my life
with your "crazy" love.
    I love you,
    J. B.
```

. . . in which he is smiling so honestly. Which I had stolen.

76

Cleaning out my closet recently I found the big business-like purse deep in a corner. It was worn now, and not as classy as I remembered it. In its only pocket, the clump of the three shoplifting tools.

I felt an old desire for something free, a present to my-self. *And it's so easy!* I thought. So, so easy, not like a risk at all.

I dressed up and took the purse to the mall, jacket over my arm, clicking the long corridors with that assured absorption, false, but convincing, and so easy to snap into again. I dallied at less-expensive stores, *like a real shopper even,* I thought, and walked into the one I'd been waiting for, the best store in the mall. The air was clean and still, and salesgirls smiled, pointed out the new arrivals. I drifted to the table of the just-in cashmere sweaters, my old favorites, so sharply folded and bright as Christmas presents under the perfect store lights. I tossed over my arm a vivid blue, a baby pink, a salmon, and a striped, grabbed a suit jacket and jeans on my way to the fitting room, and met the girl there with a plain smile. I laid the items out on the stool in the tiny room. All of this was brought in just so I could have the vivid blue sweater. I knew the salesgirl didn't even see it under the pile of other things on my arm as I brought it in.

I lifted it to my chest and looked at myself in the mirror. It was perfect, thick and soft as a dream blanket, in a blue that made my blood ache. My skin glowed next to it.

I opened the bottom of the sweater to cut out the sewn-in sensor tag on the inside seam and shoved the tag into the back pocket of the jeans I'd brought in. I pulled apart the clump of magnets, placing half on either side of the pin-tab sensor, but nothing.

No little clicks, no release. The magnets snapped back together and pinched my fingers cruelly hard.

The sensors were a new design: more plastic around the heart of its internal magnet, and in an odd teardrop shape that was difficult to keep the magnets around. They didn't stick. Not at all. They just found each other and closed back together defiantly.

I looked at myself in the mirror again. I smiled, cheered her up. I dropped the sweater back into the pile of things I didn't want, relieved.

77

I see you, Dad.
        You think no one can see you, as if the lights on you are out.

        You know, you're not wrong: the lights are out on all of us. We go on in our dark fogs. Unless someone else turns to look your way and lights the light.

78

Fifteen years after divorcing Dad, Mom got married in her hiking boots, to a steady, supportive man, the one she'd been looking for. It was just a few of us with them in a sunny park as they said their vows. A large dragonfly settled on Mom's shoulder like a brooch and stayed there until they turned to walk back to us as husband and wife. They live in a small home on a strip of land where Mom grows a giant patch of strawberries and my stepfather practices his bow and arrow on a homemade target. They go camping as often as they can.

And my sister married too. She never released me from the promise never to talk to Dad about her, where she lived or worked, or what her life was like now, so I never mentioned the wedding in my emails with him. But he found out from his siblings, who must have told him about it in their letters. Twice his recent emails mentioned it, in a slyly hurt way, saying he heard the wedding was fun and beautiful out there on the golf course, and he wished he had known about it sooner, a passive-aggressive jab at me. I recognized he was trying to manipulate me. Just as Mom said he would, and for no other reason but to make me feel a little bad, to seed our relationship with an imbalance of guilt.

But I had learned this weaponizing of pride; it had no effect on me. Instead I thought of him alone in prison, enjoying his daily distractions, but without progress, suspended in the timeless nowhere space of punishment. Suspended in betweenness.

I saw myself suspended too. My family has changed and I'm so glad for them, having evolved past him, past even his invisible reach that hung over everyone but me. And now it is everyone but me who is finished with him.

79

He loved to pretend to crash the car. We'd be driving anywhere and he'd swerve it clownishly, jolting us side to side, and we'd laugh and shriek. He'd slam the brakes and pump them twice, thumping and yelling "OH NOO, FLUFFY!" to make like he'd just run over a cat. He'd do a Donald Duck squabble and tears would stream down my face from laughing so hard.

"MOLLY LOVES YOU" he'd yell out of the car window at any random boy walking on any sidewalk as we drove by. I'd squeal and hit him and whine "Daaa-aad!," honestly embarrassed when the boy would look back at us, a classmate sometimes. I'd sink into the car seat, blushing, angry but laughing. He'd just lean again out of the window and yell louder, "MOLLY LOVES YOU!"

80

Twenty-one years went by since the first robbery and I never talked to him about it.

I saw what happened when Grandpa asked him about his motives and I assumed that would happen to me too, if I brought it up. And I didn't really want to hear what he had to say, because I didn't want the feeling of watching him lie to me ever again. He'd say the sort of stuff he said at his trials, use the logical explanations, put me on that side of things, put an official story between us.

But what did I really have to lose? I had tried everything else, everything except directly asking him to explain himself.

I wanted the real version. But I felt like the last person on the list who should be asking him about his crimes. After enough time passed I started to think he just couldn't say the real version, and who was I to deserve it anyway. And after even more time passed I started to think I already have the real version.

What was left to know? His choices are plain. Still, I wanted to know which parts were real and which parts were fake. For example, did he love Mom? It mattered to me somehow; it has something to do with the way I think about myself. If I were hurt more, I'd write him off like everyone else and just assume it was all fake, and that book would shut.

Now I'm first on the list to ask him, because I'm the only one left. I see a future where he appears again and I am there, and I don't know why. I might be the only one there. Also, I know a liar wants to be known. I know a criminal wants to be caught, because it is the only way of being known. I think a person who feels mortality sidling up wants to be known. Besides, he might be different now.

So I started there. I labored over an email to him that began with normal pleasantries and then something about getting older, and how I felt as if I was so different now from when I was in my twenties. Gingerly I transitioned into asking him about getting older, too. I asked if he felt different from before. If he ever thinks about the crimes, and if he sees them differently.

Open, nonjudgmental, baggy questions. Invitations to talk more than questions, really. I hoped with all my will he'd talk.

I checked my email every other day for weeks—no answer. A month went by, two months, three months. I figured I was cut off.

Then, a fat envelope in my mailbox. A six-page letter from him.

In the end, I don't know what I owe him. The layers of my feelings toward him seem to have no conclusion, however much I peel and dig. I don't want to say anything about this letter. It's the least I can do now, to let him speak for himself.

81

Dear Molly,

Instead of using the computer I decided to sit down and write a letter. There's a charge for email service and a half-hour time constraint. Most of the time, too, there's a waiting line for computer use—only four PCs are provided for about 150 people. I try to email early in the morning or when its mealtime and most guys are at the chow hall.

First of all, I'm glad you received that Christmas gift that Carol sent. As far as your sensitive question is concerned, I am a changed man.

My crime sprees (1994) (2009), although financially motivated, happened for different

reasons. What I understand now, however, is why
I acted impulsively and without regard to the
law. At the time I also compromised my religious
beliefs.

Back in the spring of 1994 I was apprehended
for possessing a company car and, subsequently,
GM fired me. The labor union made a deal and
I was going to be rehired after spending a
year away from GM. At the time I was renting a
condo and had credit card bills to pay. I tried
working at a couple of tool and die shops but
quit promptly—these places offered less hourly
pay and much less comfortable work conditions.

So, I decided to rob a credit union.

I got the idea of a demand note and a toy gun
from witnessing a robbery, at that same credit
union, by a young man who quietly pulled the
caper and just drove away.

When I was about to rob that Royal Oak credit
union, I told myself that I was on a paramilitary
mission and my plan had to be completed. This
attitude provided the daring and lack of
conscience that were required for committing
the crime. I believe that this attitude resulted
from my combat experience.

Since the take from the credit union robbery was
small (a few thousand), I had to continue robbing
banks in order to maintain my lifestyle—I had
custody of your sister and paid support for you.

Thus, my greatest fear was losing custody of my daughter.

After a few months I decided that I was going to commit one last crime—I had a good job offer and the winter months would be perfect to work at a small shop before returning to GM. But, I was caught, and for the first time in my life, I was locked in jail.

This experience was frightening and very uncomfortable but I hung in and was finally released in 2000. A few months after settling in at GM and in a nice apartment with your sister, I met Carol. She was different than the women I had as girlfriends. Carol was financially independent, had old-fashioned values, and most significantly, reminded me of my first wife.

When I met Carol I was not the least bit interested in meeting any women. In fact, I attended a singles dance at a church, in order to speak to a friend who had a good position at a bank and who I was hoping would help get your sister hired there.

The reason I was not interested in having another girlfriend was my criminal past—no decent woman would accept me for a meaningful relationship. Nevertheless, I pursued Carol and never told her of my crimes. She was satisfied with my response that the past is irrelevant.

Before long I was able to get a mortgage
and move to that other house with your sister.
Meanwhile, at work, the plant I worked in for
many years closed and I was moved to a building
that had very little security. As a condition
of being rehired by GM I worked the afternoon
shift. But now, at the new facility, I worked
the day shift and, like many of my coworkers, I
snuck out of the plant for hours at a time. The
Detroit casinos were opening at this time, so I
found a fun place where I spent most of my work
day.

Since I had a mortgage I was able to get
new credit cards and quickly ran up charges.
Eventually I used the cards to offset gambling
losses at the casinos.

At the same time, my relationship with Carol
blossomed and I wound up moving in with her.
My GM income was healthy but it was all used
towards a high mortgage payment, an auto loan,
multi-car insurance, and a number of credit
cards. Not to mention what I gave to you and
your sister.

In the end I fell behind on my mortgage and car
payments and misappropriated your sister's credit
card account, so I decided to retire from GM.

A $50,000 early retirement payoff covered the
money I owed your sister plus some other bills.

So, here I was, 63 years old, retired, earning
$1,700 a month from Social Security and $1,000 a
month from my pension, but I still couldn't pay
my bills. I was still gambling every day.

In January 2009 I decided to stop visiting the
casinos and I returned to a mission of stealing
money from banks so I could catch up with my
debts and finally break even. I wanted your
sister to be able to stay in that house.

As you know, my plan did not work.

I was locked up again. When this happened
I was certain that your sister would be there
for me and that Carol would be out of my life
forever. Quite the opposite happened, though. I
deceived Carol about my past (lie of omission),
her house was raided by the FBI (they smashed
the front door, confiscated her personal
property) and she was interrogated.

To my surprise, Carol forgave me for lying and
supported me after my arrest. It was then that I
learned this: had Carol known about my debts she
would have paid them off and there would have
been no need to rob banks.

This revelation changed my love for Carol.
For five years now she has waited for me. The
fact that Carol has committed herself to me has
changed me. From now on the rest of my life will
be devoted to this angel of a woman.

Thus, as far as I'm concerned, the rest of my life has a new meaning. A devoted, loving woman waits for me. We will share our remaining years together and I will also try to be a good father, grandfather, and sibling when possible.

In the interim, I'm hoping to complete this, my final time here, soon. If all goes well I'll transfer to Milan, Michigan, where I can be closer to Carol for the purpose of her visiting me. Then I'll be returning home—my real home. I'll be with Carol again.

By the way, once I'm home again, I'll continue my retirement. Perhaps I'll join Carol and we will sell birdhouses as a hobby. We are talking of becoming snow birds, do some traveling and investing in property up north.

Out of room. Hope that answers your question.

Love,

Dad

82

"These might tell you something!" Mom had written on a piece of cardboard bound with a rubber band to a few photos she wanted me to have, sent in a manila envelope covered in HAVE A NICE DAY stickers.

Thick, orangey photos with rounded corners and a far-away matte finish, photos I had never seen before, of their wedding day. Dad is wearing the gray-collared polo shirt he wore in the square portrait he'd sent to Mom. They sit together for one photo over a forest of beer and pop bottles on the table in front of them, his arm around her shoulder. Mom is the most beautiful I have ever seen her. Sharply pretty, with a perfect ruby smile like my sister's. In her eyes, a little tiredness, or drunkenness, or something worse. On her shoulder, Dad's hand is pressing hard, the gold glint of his wedding ring a bright point of light. His chin is up, eyebrows raised, mouth curling in a goofily proud grin that could be real or just kidding, I can't tell.

Another photo, a firework, a ground bloom spraying up and off to one side in the wind like a fire feather against a bank of dark apartments. No one is in that photo, just the wires of sparks, the shadows behind, and a pale evening sky.

Acknowledgments

Thank you to Blake Butler, Bill Clegg, Amy Hundley, Amy McDaniel, Kathryn Stockett, Paul and Barbara Brown, Lindsey Duvall, Christiana Worth, Ed Haworth Hoeppner, and most importantly, thank you Mom, Dad, and Boo.